DELIRIUM

DELIRIUM

An Interpretation of **Arthur Rimbaud**

Jeremy Reed

City Lights Books
San Francisco

DELIRIUM: AN INTERPRETATION OF ARTHUR RIMBAUD
© 1991 by Jeremy Reed
First City Lights edition: 1994

10 9 8 7 6 5 4 3 2 1

Cover design by Rex Ray

Library of Congress Cataloging in Publication Data

TK

City Lights Books are available to bookstores through our primary distributor: Subterranean Company. P. O. Box 160, 265 S. 5th St., Monroe, OR 97456. 503-847-5274. Toll-free orders 800-274-7826. FAX 503-847-6018. Our books are also available through library jobbers and regional distributors. For personal orders and catalogs, please write to City Lights Books, 261 Columbus Avenue, San Francisco CA 94133.

CITY LIGHTS BOOKS are edited by Lawrence Ferlinghetti and Nancy J. Peters and published at the City Lights Bookstore, 261 Columbus Avenue, San Francisco, CA 94133.

For David Gascoyne
and
Fanchon Fröhlich

That with which the public reproaches you, cultivate it: it is you.

Jean Cocteau

Contents

A. RIM·BAUD

UNE

SAISON EN ENFER

PRIX : UN FRANC

BRUXELLES
ALLIANCE TYPOGRAPHIQUE (M.-J. POOT ET COMPAGNIE)
37, rue aux Choux, 37

1873

The only book published by Rimbaud, Brussels 1873

Chapter One

In an hour it will rain. Swallows keep flickering almost at ground level in a tenacious pre-migrational grab for insects. When the rain comes the writing tension will be less acute, and some of the obsessive images which have remained with me all summer may stream off into the image forest and break up into different forms. Who and what are they? There have been red lions on my road. They sit at the entrance to the little café at which I write each afternoon. They are heat-drugged, implacably lethargic; but they have been watching me. There is this third hand, too, that comes between my right and left when I am working. And vertigo. The feeling that I am sitting on one of the revolving rings of a whirlpool, looking into its maelstromic centre. How long will it be before I get to the interior? And there are calmer images: a mountain overgrown with huge red roses, an elephant walking on a spider's-thread bridge spanning a ravine, a bay turned topaz with massed turtle shells, a blonde woman tented in a mauve towel, looking out to sea, who on turning round finds her frontal is transformed into a man's.

These image contents can be held within a visual time-frame. They are autonomous. They are personalized by my individual inner space, and belong universally to what Jung called the collective unconscious. Poets are the map-makers of the continent we call the imagination. Many have crossed it in various states of questionable repair or disrepair. Novalis in his *Hymnen an die Nacht* (Hymns to the Night), Hölderlin in the electrifying serenity of his imagined Graeco-Mediterranean cosmos, Blake in his taking it by storm, the English Romantics Coleridge, Shelley and Keats, Baudelaire in his imaginary voyages, Lautréamont in the detonative turbulence of *Maldoror*, Nerval in the hallucinated landscape of his *Aurélia*, and the schoolboy Arthur Rimbaud.

Rimbaud is my focus here. No matter how long our planet persists, Rimbaud will always be the last poet. And he is that by virtue of his flight from poetry. Jean-Nicolas-Arthur Rimbaud, the contemptuous adolescent who failed to find in poetry the physical realization of his hallucinated delirium, kicked up a dust-storm over his poetic trail. Critics are still rubbing the grit from their eyes, hoping the red blur between them and their subject will prove to be an erasable illusion. Can anyone have cared for his poetry so little? On the rough draft of 'Alchimie du verbe' Rimbaud wrote: 'Maintenant je puis dire que l'art est une sottise.' Art or poetry was too transparent. Once he had found a way of effortlessly achieving visionary expression, that is of grounding his aspiration, discovering that words can localize the infinite, poetry lost its fascination for a youth attracted to risk, to the ultimate danger of pushing the mind to the limits of its trajectory. Most of us believe that there is a limit to perception. It is when you cross it that you realize the barrier was imposed by fear. In the years between 1869 and 1873, the period in which Rimbaud believed in poetry, he seems to have been fearless in its pursuit. Youth treats the body clock with a degree of unreality. The option is open to one to believe that one may never die, or at least to think of death as an abstract notion consigned to the future. And the feeling of unlimited time and space allows one to assassinate the present. Rimbaud was briefly tyrannical because he inherited the future.

At that age I was reckless, manic, and I stole. I courted defiance because my adrenalin fed on the impulse to deconstruct that in which I believed. And the sense of violating imaginative input is made the more exciting by the fact that inspiration does not recede. It comes back the more powerful for having been abused. It is like lighting a fire and partially covering it with sand. The flame soon licks through and crackles with a wick of smoke. The poet has to maintain a suitable respect and a corresponding disrespect for the source that provides him with poetry. Rimbaud's brief years of poetic creativity are the perfect example of compliant defiance. And he was after all bored. His mother appears to have been redoubtable, draconian, narrow-minded and overcompensating for the absence of the boy's father. And that father, Frédéric Rimbaud, Captain of Infantry, cleared out when the poet was six years old, leaving behind three other children: the two girls, Vitalie and Isabelle, and Arthur's brother Frédéric. He probably left for the reasons that later prompted Rimbaud to do so: the severity of Madame Rimbaud, and the pull towards the open road. Captain Rimbaud interestingly spent some of his military career in Algeria and provided a translation into French of the Koran.

And where did Rimbaud go? As a child he escaped into the imagination; he advanced along a trajectory that swings out over the abyss. But at least there is freedom in inner space. Mooning around the house, inhaling the scent of the latrine, bored with Charleville's provincial square, sickened by those Sundays which smell of dread, and on which, holding a blue cotton umbrella, he would have to join the family's regimental procession to the eleven o'clock mass, he dreamt of freedom: anywhere but somewhere else.

Rimbaud's 'Les Poëtes de sept ans', with its presentiment of sails and voyaging into the unknown, powerfully portrays the child's sense of disgust at the asphyxiating characteristics of his home life. Maternal domination squats on the poem like a toad sitting in its own shadow. Today Rimbaud would have fed his nerves with loud music (he is in every way the prototypical punk, right to the seminal spiky hair), taken whatever drugs were available, and would have coaxed his poems towards an equally subversive millennial ethos. He would have dressed in a leather jacket and slashed denims. And there would be as much to fight against as there was in his day. Effete literary cliques, an establishment that turns epileptic whenever the imagination scalds it with current, the distillation of political poison, the conformity of the masses to material worship. A poet takes what he wants from his age; he leaves the rest to circulate like the blue-green algae which are suffocating our seas.

But what of 'Les Poëtes de sept ans'? Seven-year-old poets.

One might safely posit that if you are not writing poetry by the age of seven, you never will. Rimbaud's title carries an ironic backlash. André Breton might have lined up a procession of seven-year-old poets and had them walk through the streets of Paris to an asylum. 'Gisant au pied d'un mur, enterre dans la marne/ Et pour des visions écrasant son œil darne' ('Lying at the foot of a wall, buried in marl,/and for visions fiercely rubbing his dazzled eyes'). Rimbaud early on had realized that impacting one's fists into shut eyes generates a stream of hypnagogic imagery. It is the moment when big tropical fish nose past with such suspended fluency that one looks through a red eye into an interior in which a tiny naked girl is preoccupied with reading a poem by Rimbaud. It might be 'Le Bateau ivre', except there is no time to prolong focus, for a flotilla of chimerical shapes has entered the current. Instead of sniffing glue or a line of coke, which Rimbaud would not have been able to afford, he learnt the simple expedient of monitoring the unconscious. Rimbaud used his psychophysical body as grounds for sensory experimentation. Olfaction 'dans la fraîcheur des latrines' was one way of getting high, and later as part of Rimbaud's belief in the systematic derangement of the senses, there were to be other more sophisticated means of stimulus: starvation, drugs, alcohol and the most combustible heightener of all – the chemical components of the imagination. Rimbaud's childhood temerity instinctively sensed ways of effecting hallucination. Thrown in upon himself, pretending to read the cabbage-green edged Bible he portrays in 'Les Poëtes de sept ans', he had to devise ways of achieving a dichotomized being. Attentive on a cold December Sunday, and frozen into a spotlit exhibit by Madame Rimbaud's intrusive voyeurism, the boy had to be somewhere else, somewhere inaccessible. He had to double on himself and so the process was begun. 'Je est un autre' – 'I is another.'

And did he actually do the things he described in the poem, or were these imaginary outrages? Rimbaud lays claim to aberrations, abnormalities. He speaks of obscene gesture. He would stick out his tongue and place his two fists in his groin. He liked to converse with deformed, backward children, whose fingers were yellow and black with mud, and whose clothes stank of excrement. Olfaction seems to have been one of Rimbaud's most heightened senses; it comprised an early form of sexual gratification. And in the same poem he tells us of an encounter with an eight-year-old girl next door, who, acting rough, jumped on him, tenting him beneath her skirt. But this time the poet stringently recoils. What he experiences is not erotic fascination; his response is to bite her bottom, for she is without panties: '. . . Et qu'il était sous elle, il lui mordait les fesses,/ Car elle ne portait jamais de pantalons'. Rimbaud makes himself sound canine in this incident. If the experience was physical and not hallucinated, it suggests both the poet's savagery and his disdain for the female sex. Perhaps the pleasure for him was that she subsequently beat him black and blue. But smell is still the predominant sense, for when he returns to his bedroom he can still taste her skin: 'les saveurs de sa peau'.

Rimbaud was sixteen at the time of writing 'Les Poëtes de sept ans'; a volatile tornado of frustration and ambition was already smashing through his overstretched nerves. When there is little or nothing of the outer world to which one wishes to make claim, the inner cosmos expands. Who Rimbaud was to himself during this time is probably something so enormous, so expansively redoubtable that he was forced to restrain the imposition it made on his schizoid character. In states of extreme stress we project the opposite. The other or simulacrum is a psychopath, a twistedly malign perversion of the self. The hands confronting one may be blood-stained; the mouth open on that agonized shriek which Munch committed for all time to the history of psychopathology. Rimbaud's inner world was combustibly violent; universes were shot down into that implacable rage. And he was unremittingly hard on himself. 'I' was his experiment for the other's sadistic pleasure.

In the same month as Rimbaud wrote 'Les Poëtes de sept ans', May 1871, he wrote to his teacher Georges Izambard in tones of contemptuous familiarity:

I am cynically getting myself kept. I dig up old idiots from our school: the stupidest, dirtiest, nastiest things I can think of, is what I serve them: one is paid in beer and flesh. *Stat mater dolorosa, dum pendet filius. . . .*

Right now I am depraving myself as much as possible. Why? I want to be a poet, and I am working at making myself a *visionary*: you won't understand this at all, and I hardly know how to explain it to you. The problem is to arrive at the unknown by the derangement of *all the senses*. The suffering is enormous, but one has to be strong to be born a poet, and I have realized that I am a poet. It is not my fault. It is wrong to say: I think. Better to say: one is thought. Excuse the pun.

I is another. Too bad if a piece of wood discovers it is a violin, and to hell with those who lack this understanding and argue over something of which they are ignorant!

What interests us here is Rimbaud's concern with 'le dérèglement de *tous les sens*', and his notion of 'Je est un autre'. Rimbaud's theories castrate potential criticism because they are so flagrantly uncompromising. And they are inexpungeably individual in that they do not allow for disciples. Minor poets who are invariably distinguished by gregariousness, the need to hang out for mutual support in institutions, are not encouraged to take up with the ways of solitary genius.

And what would all this have meant to Georges Izambard? The latter had arrived in Charleville in January 1870, and at the age of twenty-one found himself in charge of the most senior literature course at the Collège. An intimate friendship based on a mutual concern for modern French poetry came about between master and pupil, and Rimbaud must have seen in Izambard the surrogate father who conformed to his homo-erotic imaginings. Denied the love and companionship of a father, Rimbaud inevitably projected the father-image on to a fortuitously chosen surrogate. Rimbaud's mother had already proved to be a disagreeable man. Her inflexible rectitude must have had the boy see her as the asexual embodiment of the punitive instinct. Could he have imagined her naked, submissive in his father's bed? Was it necessary for a woman from the Ardennes to show passion as a concomitant to sex? Did Rimbaud think he owed his origins to parthenogenesis? Adolescents can usually associate sex with most people other than their parents. In Rimbaud's case

14

the dissociation from speculating about parental conjugation must have been extreme. His mother's bed was a solitary one. A white-sheeted sarcophagus. His father at this instant might have been saddling a boy or girl in the desert. Perhaps he thought of his mother as having given birth to snakes. Four black serpents basking on the threshold, and by some slow chemical transmogrification changing into children. Arthur still had scales when he lay in the grass and dreamt of adventure.

In 'Les Poëtes de sept ans' he tells us that 'il faisait des romans sur la vie/Du grand désert, où luit la Liberté ravie,/Forêts, soleils, rives, savanes!' Rimbaud invented fictions, novels about life in the great desert, which for him represented liberty. And there was escape into forests, suns, shores and savannahs. Small wonder that Rimbaud ended up in Harrar: his inner momentum had already placed him in a mental desert. The severance with poetry that so baffles his critics had already taken place years before Rimbaud was to abandon poetry. The perversity which is manifest in his work, and which was twisted into the fibre of his sensibility, allows for no safe conclusions about anything to do with his life or art. For months I had a recurring dream in which I saw a figure, outlined against a fireball sunrise, dig a hole in the sand and set fire to a sheaf of papers. The action was done with obdurate tenacity. To renounce poetry would not have appeased Rimbaud. To destroy his creation probably would have satisfied the self-punitive disgust he attributed to almost everything he did well. It would have been his ultimate vengeance on a society he loathed. The crackle of flame; bits of ash spotting off into the air. His servant and companion, the boy Djami, could not have known the consequences of such an action. And knowing this would have heightened Rimbaud's sense of pleasure. He had changed his skin for a black one; gun-runner, slave-trader, a man preoccupied with dirty money – his ash could represent poetry to no one but himself. And yet, for all that, Djami probably knew him better than anyone. Better than Izambard, Delahaye or even Verlaine. And fittingly and thankfully Djami left no record of their love or friendship. The desert contains secrets. Rimbaud's inner life there was one of them. May the wind continue to speak of it.

And Izambard? He too knew of Baudelaire's poetry with its accent on extravagant eroticism, an existentially filtered spiritual pessimism, its morbid orchestration of a syphilitic's microphobia. It was he who introduced Rimbaud to the Parnassians, to the work of Banville, Hugo, and to Verlaine's first little books: *Les Poèmes saturniens* and *Les Fêtes galantes*. Before them were Lamartine, Nerval and the more effete Vigny. And unknown to Rimbaud, and almost contemporaneous with his own period of creativity, Isidore Ducasse, better known as Lautréamont, had already published in *Les Chants de Maldoror* a work that anticipates *Une saison en enfer*. Lautréamont's achievement is possibly the greater, for its originality and unrelenting detonation of the unconscious make it the work which more than any other precedes Freud/Jung and surrealism.

We know less of Lautréamont than we do of Rimbaud – he died in 1870 at the age of twenty-four in circumstances which have never been properly elucidated. The savagery of *Maldoror*, the brilliance of its imagery, its hallucinated bestiary which run rampant across the pages, and the vehemence with which it attacks almost every plank in the bridge on which nineteenth-century man had supposed himself secure, make it the more incendiary of the two works. Reading a line by Lautréamont is to imagine his throwing a petrol bomb at the page and racing from the scene with his clothes burning. Lautréamont assassinates both himself and his subject: unconsciously Rimbaud's time of the assassins speaks of the weird symbiosis that brought two conflagratory works into being which were to anticipate the imaginative and military holocausts of the twentieth century. Rimbaud at seventeen and Lautréamont at twenty had each put his ear to the nuclear pulse. Our potential white winter to come was for each of them a burning summer. And if they had coincided, there would have been no familiarity, no fraternity. It is possible that Rimbaud plagiarized Lautréamont: the earliest complete edition of *Les Chants de Maldoror* had been published by Lacroix, Verboeckhoven, in Brussels in 1869. Lautréamont was dead a year later. His body was found on 24 November 1870 in his hotel room at 7 Faubourg Montmartre, and no cause of death was entered on his certificate (*sans autres renseignements*). It was the winter of the Prussian siege of Paris: Lautréamont may have died from starvation, disease, suicide, or he may have been murdered. He left behind him almost no papers. *Maldoror* and *Poésies* are the two works that he bequeathed us. And like Rimbaud, Lautréamont was a refugee in inner space. Born in Montevideo, victimized by a diplomat father (it seems likely his mother committed suicide), he was sent to be educated in Tarbes, before making his way to Paris. The first *chant* of *Maldoror* had appeared as early as 1868 and made a second appearance the following year in Evariste Carrance's anthology *Parfums de l'âme.* Far more than Baudelaire's poetry, *Les Chants de Maldoror* would have excited Rimbaud to delirium. Here was a sensibility more outrageous than his own, and a poetry that knew no imposition on shock. And if Rimbaud's poetry has been the one more readily assimilated by literary taste, it is because of the two it is less savagely unorthodox.

Did it really take the surrealists to discover Lautréamont? Poetry, no matter its limited printings, has a way of filtering through to the right hands. Would not Verlaine, with his penchant for the obscene, have known of *Les Chants de Maldoror*, and could not the book have come down to Rimbaud like that – he suppressing all mention of it because it ran contemporaneous with his own discovery of a tempestuously implosive inner cosmos? Rimbaud and Lautréamont had both broken through the spatio-temporal barrier to locate the catastrophic fragmentation and volcanic insurgence rooted in the collective unconscious, that laval wave which gathering momentum was to break over the twentieth century as an accelerative hurricane.

The poet is always two people. Those who saw Rimbaud with his matted hair and urchin's clothes, kicking through the streets of Charleville or hanging out with the likes of Charles Bretagne at the Café Dutherme, could know nothing of the imaginative vision that was informing his inner world. Everything there seethed with perpetual fermentation. You can be speaking to someone about the fog outside, the local frontier guards, the contortionism of an adept prostitute, but all the time it is taking off inwards – the storm on which the poem rides. And there is a smell of singeing that accompanies it. Lines keep flashing up;

they want the whole attention they demand, and not the poet's dichotomized fade-in and fade-out of the picture. In the end there is nothing to do but run for empty space and unload the circuit.

In the same year that Lautréamont was to die, Rimbaud came to manifest his full poetic genius. During his last year at the Collège, and in part stimulated by his friendship with Izambard, Rimbaud was to put his fist through the teeth of conventional poetry. And although most English poetry has gone on pretending that Rimbaud never existed, European poetry was never to be the same again. It took a child to discover that the business of poetry is imaginative reality, the events of the inner world being hugely disproportionate in significance to those of social commentary. Most poetry which pertains to the latter is no more durable than the asterisks of rain beading the window after an abrupt shower. Rimbaud spat in the face of those who make a profession out of trivia. And today he would be playing a rakish guitar in a basement club in Berlin. He would blow the fuses on the joint and stub a cigarette into his bare shoulder. He would feed the crowd voltage and go back to his room and resume his real life, that of the subversive poet.

But that summer, the August of 1870, in the incandescent dog-days, the heat scorching the countryside around Charleville, Rimbaud struck out for Paris. It was the logical extension to poetry. The poem pushed him into exploring the physical. Its brute force had accumulated: the adrenalin banged him on to the road. The psychophysical came together as an explorative unity.

Izambard had left Rimbaud the key to his flat in the Cours d'Orléans, which meant the freedom to ransack his library; but not even this could succeed in distracting Rimbaud in a town so little conducive to his spiritual growth. He boarded a train without any money, probably not even knowing why or how he was on it, except that it was moving, and on his arrival in Paris he was arrested and taken to a police station. Locked up in the prison of Mazas, and terrified of his impending trial, he implored Izambard to help him. Interestingly he transforms his former teacher into a mother and father. 'I hope in you as in a mother', and later on in the letter he professes: 'I shall love you as a father.'

This curious gender mutation and surrogate parenthood imposed on Izambard tells us much about Rimbaud's sexual confusion. Perhaps in his imagination he regularly had Izambard change sex according to his need for him as feminine or masculine, unrealized lover or mentor. What is most fascinating about Rimbaud's creative years, in terms of sexual orientation, is that they are unfocused. His interest in women is confined to smut and scatology, and his attraction to men is based on cruelty and brutality, and certainly not eroticism. Even Verlaine is a figure to be used in an experiment, and part of Rimbaud's attraction to Verlaine centred upon wrecking the latter's domestic stability and driving him towards a visionary liberation from which the lesser poet was unlikely to benefit. Verlaine's perfect ear and the transparency of his lyric were the consummate gifts of a minor poet. No amount of forcing his sensibility or deranging his sensory perception was ever going to make him into a seer, a frenzied shaman. For Rimbaud hallucination was a way of seeing. So it is with all great imaginative poets. And while that particular faculty may be stimulated, it cannot be inherited. Rimbaud was disappointed by hashish. He saw a white moon chasing a black one across the sky. The image would have been too ordinary to have fitted into his poetry.

Rimbaud's great battles were fought on the inner plane, the arena in which the poet contests with light and dark, truth and shadow, self and double. 'Le combat spirituel est aussi brutal que la bataille d'hommes; mais la vision de la justice est le plaisir de Dieu seul' ('Spiritual battle is as brutal as man's wars; but the vision of justice is God's pleasure alone'), he asserts in *Une saison en enfer*. The cosmos lives in the poet's interior. It is there that one is attentive to the roar of space. All the processional chimeras, black angels, psychopomps, archetypal tableaux, erotic possibilities, beauty, mutilation, visions of past and future worlds are contained within the geography of the unconscious. Rimbaud was in a quite different country to Verlaine, no matter that they both experienced kicks from being physically on the road.

19

Rimbaud's first flight to Paris involved imprisonment. Punishment for being a poet was not new to him; his mother's relentless severity had already impressed on him that impracticality was a luxury incompatible with her peasant blood. Her brothers were hard-drinking alcoholics. Brought up as she had been on a farm in Roche, whose meagre soil yielded indifferent harvests, and having assumed since her mother's early death responsibility for her brothers and sister, Vitalie Cuif, the future Madame Rimbaud, was little disposed to have an itinerant son whose scholarly acumen was being visibly dissipated in the pursuit of poetry. 'Work is further from me than my fingernail is from my eye. Shit for me,' Rimbaud was to write to Verlaine. 'When you see me positively eat shit, only then will you find how little it costs to feed me.' To Vitalie Rimbaud her son's defiant, truculent disobedience was to be viewed as an unpardonable aberration. But it was worse than that, for the resolution that he had set himself – to become a poet – was an inner conviction she was powerless to reach. Smacking his face, humiliating him, confining him to the house, treating him as a delinquent, none of these punitive measures could get inside him. Vitalie Rimbaud came face to face with the impenetrable existential wall that prevents one person having access to another's inner life. It is no good shrieking 'What are you thinking?' or picking someone up by their hair, there is simply no way through. We are all solitaries situated somewhere in a space that we cannot locate. Where are we in relation to body space? Consciousness tells us nothing. It is what? The precondition to being. Wherever Rimbaud was, no one in his life seems ever to have come close to it. His psychic outback extended to Mars.

When Rimbaud took flight from Charleville for the second time, and in a country still at war, it was to set out on foot for Brussels. It was now October 1870 with its gold fall of autumn leaves, that month in which the light stays in the trees like filtered honey. The Franco-Prussian War had broken out in August, the month of his disastrous visit to Paris. Rimbaud must have felt poetry was an invincible protector, for his vulnerability on the road and lack of any financial provision were serious liabilities. But he was intoxicated by danger. Pushing himself to extremes, going without food, sleeping out in vermin-infested clothes were stages of induction towards his confrontation with visionary experience. His mind must have been massive with expectation. The roads were dust; but there was the exhilaration of sudden showers sparkling across the landscape. He would have heard the shrieking of jays, busy collecting acorns, the branch-shaking gymnastics of squirrels. He was free. Somewhere along the road, half buried on the slope of a valley swollen with watercress, was the dead soldier who found his way into 'Le Dormeur du val'. And Rimbaud was insatiably curious. Surely he would have dropped down into the valley to examine the corpse? He would have stolen whatever money, valuables or tobacco he could find in the man's blood-soaked uniform. There had to be something he could sell to finance his journey. He went through Charleroi on his way to Brussels, where he begged shelter and food from an acquaintance of Izambard's. Poems like 'Les Effarés', 'Au Cabaret-Vert', 'Le Mal', 'Rages de César' and 'Le Dormeur du val' all owe their inspiration to this second truancy from home.

Did he sell his body on the way? Probably not. On his next flight to Paris he was to be raped, or more to the point gang-banged by the military. This time the elated pantheism he was near to experiencing in 1870 provided him, despite his close proximity to starvation, with an adrenalized dynamic of energy. He was nervously charged like a thief before he steals. And isn't there in Rimbaud's childhood behaviour the premonition of the young vagrant, Jean Genet, who was likewise to adopt a psychology of wilful self-debasement in the pursuit of imaginative truth?

Rimbaud was looking for something he could not locate or yet express in the visionary language which so eloquently informs 'Le Bateau ivre', *Les Illuminations* and his 'Negro Book' – *Une saison en enfer*. The alchemical process had begun. He knew he was marked. Something he could not properly apprehend was growing in him. He must have wondered why he, the child of undistinguished parents and a provincial schoolboy, should be the messenger to what he hoped would be a future race. What could that mean to those from whom he had to beg? How do you declare yourself as an evolutive visionary? The dirt on his face, his straggly hair, his broad, red fingers must have had people assume he was bad blood on the run from home. All he knew was that the tempestuous momentum of his poetic vision forced him out into the open. What is in most young men a prompting sanctioned by sexual curiosity, so that instinctively one strays into alleys and places where sex may be realized, was in Rimbaud the desire to find the physical location that corresponded to his psychic locus. And in the process the ordinary is transformed into the marvellous. You can be looking at a door-frame from which the paint is flaking, the windowless, dead side of a building – any building – and quite suddenly it is there. A line of poetry has intersected with an incongruous external. The two are not related, but the juxtaposition was necessary to generate the tension needed for the writing of a poem.

Rimbaud picked up things with his eye on this journey. Seeing is not only a continuous visual retrieval but a form of unmonitored theft. You can raid both things and people. One can appropriate whatever catches the eye, and on a sexual plane masturbation is the means of making love to an involuntary image. Poetry is close to the latter in its function. One can internalize any woman or man of one's choice, in Rimbaud's case it was probably both, and it is the same with poetry. One sensitizes the idea of a thing, frictionalizes it with one's nerves and transforms it into something else. Poetry is the most sophisticated form of psychophysical masturbation. In writing poetry one does not achieve the object of one's desire; one compromises for an approximation. The end product is elusive, it evades the perceiver in the same way as the imagined sexual fantasy blurs in the act of retaining it.

Rimbaud's poem 'Au Cabaret-Vert', written most probably on the road to Charleroi in October 1870, is impregnated with an autumnal calm. It is a poem of late sunshine. It expresses a mood one associates with Rimbaud that autumn. It is the calm before the storm; the achievement of a poetry which, while it disdains comfortable emotion or social acceptance, none the less expresses a containable tension within the poet. And a sense of placement: he has no need to counter-attack his line, for the poem follows his physical routing. And Rimbaud, who expressed

22

such temerity on a spiritual plane, manifests an almost voyeuristic awkwardness in his real or imagined notice of girls encountered on the way. In 'Au Cabaret-Vert' it is 'the girl with the huge tits' and the obvious sexual experience – 'a kiss wouldn't scare that one' – who serves him with the simple dish of bread and butter and ham. The simplicity of his needs, so unselfconsciously portrayed in the poem, right down to his beer-froth turning gold in the late sunshine, has the serene properties of certainty; something that sexual intrusion would have shattered. 'Au Cabaret-Vert' isolates a mood. It finds Rimbaud emulating adults; he is at ease in a country inn, although no doubt tongue-tied, occupying a corner by himself and viewing the company with modified paranoia. The money for his food may have come from the pockets of a dead soldier. Rimbaud would have appreciated that irony. But there is more than a mood to this poem: there is a flippancy and a customary shade of his familiar contempt. 'For eight days I'd ripped my boots up on the road,' he tells us in the poem. And certainly his mother wasn't going to replace them. When his clothes went to tatters they stayed that way. He cultivated lack of hygiene and a vagrant's appearance. He seems all the time to have been going against himself, pushing his perversity to see how far he could injure the sensitive person within. He may never have intended to go to violent extremes, to follow to the end of the night in search of the midnight sun, but at some stage it got out of control. It was too late to reverse the syndrome. The I had literally become the other.

But it is still October 1870. Rimbaud wanted to change the world. The orthodox hegemony of material greed and the conformist masses subjugated to its ethic held little attraction for a young man whose life was already that of a poet. And it hadn't changed in October 1990. The poet remains an outsider who threatens the capitalist ethos. The world of business, politics and journalism slams iron doors in the face of imaginative truth. Inner space is a proscribed sanctuary. It is thought to be dangerous to go there; man must compute his bank balance and raise his arm in salute to International Commerce.

But in those autumn weeks of ripping his boots up, taking in the last of the sun's diminishing warmth, and writing poems which, while they hint at sex, remain on a level of mental curiosity, Rimbaud was marking time. In 'La Maline' it is again a servant-girl who he imagines teases him into kissing her. There is a pink and white peach-bloom on her cheeks. She too is a child disguised as a woman: 'En faisant, de sa lèvre enfantine, une moue' ('And pouting with her childish mouth'). He can feel comfortable in her presence, for each recognizes in the other the adoptive role of the adult.

The poem 'Ma bohème', from the same group written in October 1870, is an autobiographical finger-sketch of how Rimbaud saw himself at the time. 'Je m'en allais, les poings dans mes poches crevées;/ Mon paletot aussi devenait idéal' ('I ran off, my fists in my torn pockets;/ My overcoat too was growing ideal'). His threadbare appearance was a way of rejecting his mother's concern with bourgeois standards of dress. It was like taking her face to pieces each time another seam was torn or another finger holed the lining.

The photograph we have of Rimbaud at the time of his First Communion, when he was eleven, depicts the boy wearing the black jacket and home-made slate-blue trousers, together with the starched white shirt, that his mother had painstakingly prepared. But his boots, despite the attempt to polish them, are worn into leather wrinkles. Rimbaud was hard on shoes because he walked; he needed that physical momentum in order to air his inner ferment. But there is already someone far older sitting behind his eyes. Someone who has taken the boy by surprise. Extreme vulnerability and extreme contempt meet as an insoluble contradiction. The pose for the photographer's slow release is enforced, but the boy has been unable to settle into a state of composure. No matter his resolution at this age to accept Christianity, the rebel within him is basking in corners. Later on this vulpine presentiment will stretch its sinewy body, show its wolf's red eyes and prick up its ears. It is waiting for the time of the assassins.

In the lazy autumn light of October 1870 Rimbaud enjoyed the last sensations of innocence to permeate his childhood. His precocity, his obscenity, his disrespect for adults whatever their station in life had whipped up a fire of rebellion in him, which was to be fanned to a visionary heat in the course of the next three years.

The gold light was an interlude. Izambard was sent to Brussels, found Rimbaud at Douai, and from there he returned to Charleville in the company óf a police officer. How he must have dreaded the reception that awaited him at home. His hatred of his mother was increased by the way he could mentally mutilate her. She was powerless to efface his effigial imaginings. Perhaps he saw her as a one-eyed, square-bodied ogre blocking the entrance to his street. He could do anything to her; mastectomize her, run up the cliff-face of her body to plant a flag in her skull, or he could imagine her shrunk to something so small she would sit in a mousehole begging for crumbs of cheese.

But the journey was worth it for the poems and the sense of spiritual liberation that Rimbaud experienced whenever he was on the road. In poems like 'Le Mal' and 'L'Eclatante Victoire de Sarrebrück', the latter inspired by a brilliantly coloured Belgian print, Rimbaud picks up on the spirit of war raging in the French countryside. In 'Le Mal' his outrage at authoritarian institutions – the Army and the Church – and his compassion for those butchered in the name of territorial avarice, finds powerful expression. 'Tandis qu'une folie épouvantable broie/En fait de cent milliers d'hommes un tas fumant;/ – Pauvres morts! dans l'été, dans l'herbe, dans ta joie,/ Nature! ô toi qui fis ces hommes saintement! . . .' ('While a ravening madness triturates/And heaps a hundred thousand men into a pyre;/ Poor victims! in summer, in the grass,/ As nature's own, weren't these intended joy. . . .')

But it is in 'Le Dormeur du val' that we both see and feel the poet's presence. The poem operates on a taut thread, and if it comes out on the side of compassion, it is because the dead soldier is young. It is almost as if Rimbaud is looking for the last time at the child he has to relinquish in order to become the embodiment of the suprahuman *voyant*; and that valediction is symbolized by the open-mouthed, bloodied corpse that lies sprawled in the blue watercress. The imagination at work here is not hallucinated, but it is heightened. It is one of Rimbaud's early poems in which one feels the subject has an external existence.

In the green hollow in which the poem exists, a clear stream crazily reproduces itself in silver tatters through the grasses. The valley bubbles with light. Rimbaud is filthy. He needs to wash his dirt-encrusted hands and he desperately needs money. It is not theft to steal from yourself. And this boy-soldier dead in the floating cresses is suddenly Rimbaud's other. He can believe it in the frenzy of rolling down the slope to meet up with the stream, his fall broken with his customary exclamation of multiple Shits! '. . . la lumière pleut,' he tells us. The light rains. The green, liquid refraction of the valley makes the light suggest that it is fluid. The soldier has his feet stuck in gladioli. At first, Rimbaud starts, thinking the person is asleep. He probably pulled up short of the dead body. But the angle of his mouth, which resembles that of a sick child's, is unmistakably the loose-jawed expression which comes with death. Rimbaud is terse. 'He is cold.'

Life and death are big issues to a schoolboy alone in a valley in which shots have been exchanged. And with his obsessive olfactory command, Rimbaud notes: 'Les parfums ne font pas frissonner sa narine' ('There is no odour which can make the dead man's nostrils quiver'). And if the soldier simulates sleep, one hand placed on his chest, there are still 'two red holes in his right side'.

When Rimbaud made it back up the slope, still panting with shock and excitement, he had effectively buried the child in him. Who knows if, looking back in the course of his expansively undisciplined itineraries, he didn't identify with this place? See it again in the diffused white light? But it is always later. He was soon to be someone else. He had lived and known the experience. It was time to clear off in the direction of madness.

Chapter Two

And madness is an actual place. It is a state of mind; but it is also a location. What goes on happens at a different speed, in a dislocated sequence, and is detached from time. Most poets visit that house. It may be a square, black building in the middle of the desert. A woman with her hair in flames and a sunflower between her legs reclines on the roof-top. Her hair will never stop burning. When a cloud drifts over, it is square like a building block. Two eyes stare from it as in the portrait of a rectangular face.

In less than a year after he was taken back to Charleville in October 1870, Rimbaud was to make further, more extensive flights to Paris. He was to be raped, he was to participate in the Commune, write 'Le Bateau ivre' and his extraordinary Lettres du voyant, and finally, in the late summer of 1871, to end up on Verlaine's doorstep.

Poetic madness demands a cyclonic inner revolution. Poets who accept the external world as the singular premise for descriptive creation, live without ever generating the momentum necessary to take off into inner space. Poetry is like ballistics. The poem is a missile pointing from its launching-pad to the intergalactic archipelagos of inner space. And in the manner of a shaman Rimbaud used to slash his body with knives. Cuts into his chest both stimulated his senses and invited his usual curiosity as to how far he could go. Later on he was to have German-style knife duels with Verlaine, in which each would wrap a sharp blade in a towel with only the tip showing and aim at the other's face or throat. A police report dated 1 August 1873 states: 'These two individuals fought and tore at one another like wild beasts, just for the pleasure of making it up afterwards.' One can imagine Verlaine drunk, hysterical, vituperative, and Rimbaud cool, obscene, lacerating – the more likely of the two to have inflicted incisions.

Most people fear madness: they do not know what it comprises, but something within instinctively warns them against any encounter with the ecliptic chimera. They have a premonition of what madness could be: an involuntary loss of control, driving with no hands on the wheel; a blank space in which no coherent thought leads to another.

Nerval's journeys to the Orient and Baudelaire's metaphysical voyages were starting-points to reach the other shore. The physical world was too readily exhaustible. Remonstrating against ennui, Baudelaire had proclaimed: 'Plonger au fond du gouffre, Enfer ou Ciel qu'importe?/ Au fond de l'inconnu trouver du nouveau.' The emphasis here on finding the new – and Rimbaud would have construed this place as a psychologically constellated state – had for Rimbaud the effect of shooting up on speed. He would take heaven by storm; and if he failed, he would gladly turn to the dark. Interestingly, it is Novalis in his *Hymen an die Nacht* who anticipates the mystic expectation of the new world to which Rimbaud aspired. Novalis writes:

Now I know when the last morning will be – when the light will no longer intrude on night and love – and when sleep will always become one uninterrupted dream. My pilgrimage to the holy grave was exhausting; the cross unmanageable. The crystal wave, inaudible to lesser senses, wells up in the hill's dark hollow, at the foot of which the terrestrial tide ebbs, and whoever tastes it, whoever has stood on the world's threshold and looked over into the promised land into the night's dwelling, truly that person will not return to the ways of the world, and to the place where light is in a state of perpetual unrest.

Rimbaud had already renounced the ways of the world. As he

kicked around that winter in the Charleville woods, smoking his short pipe with the bowl turned downwards, chalking up on walls or park benches *Death to God*, or hiding out in an abandoned quarry shaft in a wood near Romeny and Le Theux, his mind was beginning to fire with the visionary impulse. The over-stimulus of adrenalin in his body – and it is physiologically arguable that a poet is characterized by adrenal debris not assimilated by the kidneys – took on in Rimbaud the nature of an excitable obscenity. He spoke of screwing dogs – whatever bitch strayed into his territory – and no doubt made similar boasts about fellatio. With his mind already flexing for new worlds, the body must have appeared as limited to him in its sexual functions as it did to de Sade.

If Rimbaud was formulating a literary theory at this time, and he gives the impression that systematic thought and mental schemas were of little interest to him (like Hart Crane he read for sensation and not knowledge), it was to evolve in the letters sent to Georges Izambard on 13 May 1871 and two days later on 15 May to Paul Demeny. Rimbaud had travelled a long way through mental space to arrive at his beliefs, and if he picked up snatches of alchemy and magic from the likes of Michelet and Eliphas Levi, and if his imagination was coloured by the works of Baudelaire, Hugo, Poe, Jules Verne and the contemporaries in whom he expressed interest, Banville, Demeny, Verlaine, Armand Renaud and Louis Veuillot, then his visionary quest is all the more original, for it is inspired not by a synthesis of literary study but by a rejection of everything that had come before him.

Poets of Rimbaud's nature do not have time to read books in the meticulous way that scholars do. A poet makes a raid on the imagery, reads for sense stimulus and for whatever characteristics in the work that can be of help to him. This method of intuitive reading means that a book can be quintessentially evaluated by random lines, random pages. A poem that appears to owe its root origins to a particular book, may in fact be indebted to little more than one haphazardly encountered image. One perception leads directly to another. In the winter of 1870/1 Rimbaud was not reading to acquire knowledge; he was looking to fan the excited nebulae that had grown up in his unconscious with associations which might help to spark off poems.

Moreover, some time in the spring of 1871, on one of his audacious flights to Paris, he had been raped. Wanting to enlist in the army of the Communards, and at the same time curious about sex, he may have invited the violation by hanging around one of the Paris barracks. He may have been mistaken for a street-boy looking to sell his body. The experience gave rise to the poem 'Le Cœur volé', and the psychological scar inflicted by rape clearly increased the poet's intention to avenge himself on society through writing that would carry the occult potency of ritual magic.

'Le Cœur volé' is explicit in terms of somatic revulsion. The poem anticipates Artaud's obsession with turning the body inside out as the sounding-board for a pain transmitted to the poetic line. 'Mon triste cœur bave à la poupe,/ Mon cœur couvert de caporal:/ Ils y lancent des jets de soupe' ('My poor heart dribbles at the poop,/ My heart soiled with cigarette-spit:/ They spatter it with jets of soup'). And in the second stanza he describes the coarsely erect soldiers. They are ithyphallic, obscene, they jeer as he is buggered. There is no respite when you are impaled. Not even the childlike invention of the magic word 'abracadabratic', in relation to the waves which he hopes will wash over and purify his defiled body, can be of any assistance. He tells us that the aftermath will be stomach retchings – 'J'aurai des sursauts stomachiques' – for the men have clearly used him violently. He was probably booted back on the street, alone, where he was unable to find any consolation for this degrading experience amidst the anonymous lives pouring through the city. Paris was in a state of insurrection; the sodomizing of a young tramp up from the provinces would have been the subject of ridicule and not investigation. What else could a boy expect if he hung around soldiers?

Whether Rimbaud actually participated in the Commune, fighting with the insurgent army against the Versaillais, who represented the elected government, we do not know. His wild rage was being directed inwardly. To the external world he was nothing; a schoolboy turned ruffian, a subversive idler to those who recognized him in Charleville. But he was preparing a lycanthropic attack. The poetry that Rimbaud was writing at the time of his *Lettres du voyant* is often obscene and violently denigratory of women. Rimbaud's mother petrified him: she was Medusa? Were they all like that? Sympathetic women had not entered into Rimbaud's life, and one senses that throughout his youthfully vehement poetic rebellion he partly blames women for his inverted sexuality and for the vulnerability to which he is exposed. And hadn't he been raped? Why was one given no protection? The soldiers had used him as a substitute for a girl. His sixteen-year-old world was upside-down. His method was to lash out; he would reduce sex to scatology, to canine bestiality.

In 'L'Orgie parisienne' written in the early summer of 1871, Rimbaud envisaged Paris as a sprawling, scabrous whore. His fury mounts attack after attack on the image of copulation.

> O cœurs de saleté, bouches épouvantables,
> Fonctionnez plus fort, bouches de puanteurs!
> Un vin pour ces torpeurs ignobles, sur ces tables . . .
> Vos ventres sont fondus de hontes, ô Vainqueurs!

> O filthy hearts, stinking mouths,
> Work up a rhythm, breathing stench
> Pour wine, for these depraved tables . . .
> Your bellies melt with shame, o Conquerors!

There is worse to come. One can feel how Rimbaud whips himself into a state of dementia.

> Parce que vous fouillez le ventre de la Femme,
> Vous craignez d'elle encore une convulsion
> Qui crie, asphyxiant votre nichée infâme
> Sur sa poitrine, en une horrible pression.

> Because you rummage through a woman's guts,
> You fear from her another convulsion
> Her crying out, that stifles your lewd perch
> Asserting perverse pressure on her breasts.

31

For Rimbaud 'L'Orgie parisienne' was a form of counter-rape. Humiliated, and too poor to combat the injustices meted out to him in the capital, he turns the city into an intestinal metaphor. This was his power. Poetry was a method of lashing his enemies with Sadean thongs. Even if the welts were visible only to posterity, he would still lay deep cuts. And at this stage of his adolescent career he had not yet extinguished the notion of literary ambition. If his age seemed a detriment to his aspirations, his inner conviction that he was a true poet and that the older generation of living poets were to be vilified as expendable fossils, served as an additional obstacle. All of Rimbaud's creative life is like this. The wave on which he surfs is invariably opposed by a counter-momentum, so that he throws himself board and all at the beach in a state of exalted surprise, only to run up the face of the outgoing wave. Rimbaud's progress creates an equal valency of obstruction. It is this process of counterbalancing tensions which gives a Rimbaud poem the force of a fire started by an arsonist, engulfing the building as well as himself. Rimbaud smashes up poetic furniture in the way that a drunk, turned violent, takes the bottom out of a chair on a man's head.

Rimbaud's psychic discoveries, his attunement to the brutally objective power that the poet turns on his subjectivity, was building to delirium in the spring and summer months of 1871. He had succeeded on several occasions in putting Charleville behind him in terms of physical space; but the place sat on his back like the shell of a turtle. In his need he returned to it; a pattern that he was to follow for the rest of his life. It was after all home, no matter that he despised it. The incongruity for him must have lain in the improbable likelihood that a great poet could originate from a provincial backwater. He adopted arrogance as a cover for excessive anxiety. He was building towards 'Le bateau ivre', his great navigable journey across imaginary seas.

Something of Rimbaud's necessary heartlessness at this time is recounted by his friend Ernest Delahaye. When the two young men were walking past the stud-farms at Mézières, which had been converted into a hospital camp for victims of the Franco-Prussian War, they caught sight of casualties who were missing arms and legs. Rimbaud, who was little disposed to his friend's compassion for the maimed, declared: 'Those loonies were simply the instruments of the defunct regime. As long as they were thought to be the stronger, they were praised. Look at them now. They wear cotton caps and are half dead – what do you expect to be done with them?'

Presumably Rimbaud thought the same of most living poets. They were and are in most cases debris left behind by the old century rather than innovators reaching forward to the new one. Rimbaud lit a forest fire around them. His poetry singularly extinguished an entire century's poetics, with the exception of Baudelaire, Nerval, Lautréamont and a little of Verlaine. Progress demands this sort of corrosive fury. Invention is contingent on disrespect. Rimbaud sensed with an unerringly sanguine instinct that literary movements owe their success to playing safe. The public want to be assured of their own psychological limitations; they want art to endorse a sense data that corresponds to the ordinary. Rimbaud knew he had the measure of such stupidity, even if the detonation rang true long after he had disowned an interest in poetry.

Rimbaud's two letters, Lettres du voyant, no doubt written quickly and under pressure of immediate inspiration, are the beginnings of a new dawn of poetry. He announces the arrival of the assassins. These two letters, the second enlarging and expanding on the theories developed in the first, are of such profound significance that they could have altered both the course of poetry and the future of the race, if they had issued from the pen of someone other than an insignificant provincial schoolboy.

The first of the Lettres du voyant was written by Rimbaud to his former teacher, Georges Izambard, and is dated 13 May 1871. I have already quoted the parts which deal with the self-induced derangement of the senses as an initiatory rite to vision. But as important to this letter is the snarling contempt that Rimbaud reveals for his teacher's concern that he should conform both in his poetry and in his professional life to the social dictates of respectability. Rimbaud launches his theory in opposition to Izambard's bias towards safety. His tone is insolent, his manner menacing; he is already quite sure that the recipient of his letter will never take to the visionary impulse.

> . . . Basically, all you see in your principle is subjective poetry: your obstinacy in going back to the university trough – excuse me – proves it. But you will always end up self-satisfied without ever having done anything, because that was your wish. Not to mention that your subjective poetry will always be disgustingly insipid. One day, I hope – as many others do – I shall see objective poetry in your principle, and see it more sincerely than you! – I shall be a worker: that is the idea which constrains me when mad rage drives me towards the battle of Paris – where so many workers are dying as I write to you! Work now, never, never; I am on strike.

Rimbaud's impatience with insipid poetry, his attack on the self-indulgent sentimentality or subjectivity of Izambard's verse, becomes in the second letter a fulmination against 'countless idiotic generations'. The 'mad rage' that Rimbaud describes as subverting his passion to become involved in the battle of Paris, was the furnacing chaos within him cooling to visionary lucidity. He is a 'worker' in the name of poetic vision. To have arrived at where one is in poetry entails mental aeons of unconscious activity. The atemporal functionings of the imagination, inheriting as it does archetypes, myth, reincarnational experience, and delivered in intermittent and blinding flashes, injected into Rimbaud at this time a visionary cosmogony quite disproportionate to his age and worldly knowledge. Poets who rely wholly on the acquisition of empirical data are those whose impetus dries up in a middle-age drought. Visionary poetry is inexhaustible, for it picks up on the rhythm of the cosmos. Meteors chase through the poet's head.

It is in the second of the Lettres du voyant that Rimbaud offers his fullest and most impassioned commitment to an uncompromising poetic delirium. Written two days after the first letter, the beliefs he expresses have ignited in his nerves.

Rimbaud begins his letter – dated 15 May 1871 and addressed to Paul Demeny – by cutting history down to size, reducing the redoubtable forest to firewood. With a smack of justifiably imperious condescension he announces:

> ... All ancient poetry culminated in the Greek, harmonious Life. – From Greece to the romantic movement – in the Middle Ages – there are writers, and versifiers. From Ennius to Theroldus, from Theroldus to Casimir Delavigne, it is all rhymed prose, a game, degradation and glory of countless idiotic generations. Racine alone is pure, strong, great. – If his rhymes had been liquidated, and his hemistiches mixed up, today the Divine Fool would be as little known as any old author of *Origins*. – After Racine, the game gets rusty. It has been going on for two thousand years!

Whether or not Rimbaud had read the authors whom he quotes, his assumptions ring vitally true. Dead poetry, fossil poetry, Racine's mechanical couplets, Rimbaud saw that all these things remained an impediment to poetic progress. Lacking inner dynamism and a conflict worked out through the opposition of irreconcilables, most poetry by the mid-nineteenth century had devolved into 'rhymed prose', in the manner that most of the bad poetry written today goes under the banner of free verse, while it is in fact prose arbitrarily truncated to make the line lengths appear to conform to poetic structure. Rimbaud is not only intent on shocking, but he is deadly serious in his aim to invent a new poetics, something he was to achieve in the prose poems of *Les Illuminations*, and in much of the writing that makes up *Une saison en enfer*.

One can imagine Rimbaud spitting in the process of writing this last letter. His thoughts raced too fast. It was hot, and he was probably uncomfortable in his dirty clothes. What could his mother have to do with this? She wouldn't have understood a line. His potential was suddenly before him; it moved jerkily like a series of film stills not yet edited into a sequence. The part of his mind not concentrating on the page was probably devising ways of getting drinks in the local cafés. His friend Bretagne would see to that later. When he takes the letter up again it is to attack those for whom writing is an ego-dominated experience:

'If those old idiots had not discovered only the false meaning of the Ego, we shouldn't have to sweep away the millions of skeletons which, since time immemorial, have accumulated the results of their one-eyed intelligence, by claiming to be the authors!'

Before arriving at the inspired prescriptions necessary for the poet to become a visionary, an inhabitant of the great dream, Rimbaud cleans the past like a fish. Men are still awaiting the arrival of a poet. 'Pen-pushers, civil servants: author, creator, poet, that man never existed!' Even Baudelaire, whom Rimbaud called 'king of poets', had advanced and withdrawn from the edge. Rimbaud, like an astrophysicist in the twentieth century, was about to release the blueprints for ecstatic mental flight. The dervish, the shaman, the assassin intoxicated by hashish, would have understood his demands. It is right to be 'monstrous' he asserts: 'Think of a man implanting and cultivating warts on his face.' His assertions are unequivocable.

The Poet makes himself a *seer* by a long, prodigious and systematized *derangement* of *all the senses*. All forms of love, suffering, and madness; he searches himself, he consumes all poisons in himself and keeps only their quintessences. Unspeakable torture in which he needs self-conviction and superhuman strength, where he becomes among all men the great invalid, the great criminal, the great outlaw – and the Wise Man! – Because he attains the *unknown*! Because he has cultivated his soul, already rich, more than anyone! He reaches the unknown, and even if, demented, he ends up losing the meaning of his visions, at least he has seen them! Let him die as he forces through unheard of, unnameable things: other horrible workers will come; they will begin at the horizons where the first one collapsed!

Rimbaud's imperatives are unprecedentedly revolutionary. They demand a commitment to the work and a willingness to explore all facets of human experience, such as few poets have ever dared contemplate. If you need a fix of heroin, and Rimbaud's demands are no less extreme, you may have to sell your body to pay for your habit. If you are a poet, you may have to steal to live. You become 'the great criminal', not only in the sense of aspiring to occult knowledge but in the context of living outside society. At the time that Rimbaud was formulating his belief in poetic dementia, and the fearless journeying to the interior where man must alchemically distil his emotions, extracting only what is of use to the experiment, poetry was comfortably in the hands of the safe. Banville, Hugo, Tennyson and Arnold, not to mention Longfellow, were all busy writing a poetry that conformed to public sentiment. Rimbaud's discoveries would have appeared an act of madness to their retrograde conformism.

Rimbaud strikes like a wolf aiming for the throat. Only Nietzsche would have understood his ecstatic celebration of evil as an objective contributory to creative vision. And the poet must be willing to accept death as the outcome of his Promethean raid on the inarticulate. The latter is a small price to pay for the incandescent immediacy of having seen and known the high points of visionary crystallization.

Rimbaud swallowed fire. He was a magician who used his psychophysical responses as a bridge across the universe. He was at this time an ecstatic savant. He was Prometheus inciting the retribution that comes from stealing fire.

At the time of writing this second May letter, 'we found him too gloomy, too irascible; his movements were jerky, his manners crude. His mother was desperate about him: at one point, he seemed so strange that she thought he was mad', writes Paterne Berrichon.

Rimbaud continues the letter to Demeny with growing excitement and a sense of corresponding intolerance.

Therefore the poet is really the thief of fire.

He is responsible for humanity, even for the *animals*; he will have to have his visions smelt, felt and heard; if what he brings back from *down there* has form, he gives it form; if it is formless, he leaves it like that. A language must be found; – Besides, all speech is idea, the time of a universal language will come! One has to be an academic – more dead than a fossil – to compile a dictionary, no matter the language. Weak-minded people, beginning *by thinking* about the first letter of the alphabet, would quickly go mad!

This language will be of the soul for the soul, containing everything, smells, sounds, colours, thought contesting thought. The poet would define the amount of the unknown awakening in his time in the universal soul: he would provide more – than the formulation of his thought, than the record *of his march towards Progress!* Enormity becoming normal, absorbed by everyone, he would really be *a multiplier of progress!*

Rimbaud's Promethean assertions which adhere to the romantic credo that creation is synonymous with death, and that one involves the other, are here translated into a context of total artistic revolution. Vision demands new sensory responses; its existence in poetry asks that it appeals to all the senses: smell, touch, hearing and so forth. These synaesthetic qualities, which will afford poetry a universal language, are achieved by a journey undertaken *là-bas* – down there. And Rimbaud had already spent a lot of time staring into the void. The poet carries the pit inside him; all manner of violent disturbance has to be encountered in the exploration of the shadow, and what is retrieved may have form or not. What is important is that it is not discounted from poetry on any moral pretext. And the poet's discoveries will require the new language, of which Rimbaud warns that madness will ensue should it be encountered by the unprepared. Rimbaud's notion of language is cabalistic, orphic, alchemical; it pivots on the individual symbolism contained by words through their component letter and number valencies. Language is breath: and poetry is the occult manifestation of that rhythm. The poet, says Rimbaud, is 'responsible for humanity, even for the *animals*'. His words should animate the universe. He should be able to interpret the communication of all creatures. The poet is the one through whom the universe vibrates. In Rimbaud, the distinction between self and world, individual and differentiated objects is broken down. Most poetry is written with the notion that the subjective responds to objective phenomena. Rimbaud hastens to rectify this misconception.

Why was his mother desperate about him at this time? It is

unlikely that he had access to drugs in Charleville – this was to come later in Paris – but clearly his aberrations had become ungovernable. Did he interfere with his sisters? Did his mother catch him masturbating? As a behaviour trait in Paris, he excreted into his host's milk bottle. It is possible he did the same at home. But there had also been trouble with his former teacher Georges Izambard. Ever since Rimbaud had sent Izambard 'Le Cœur volé', with its undisguised admission of homosexuality, a wedge had come between the two; a division which was to prove final. Izambard had written in response to Rimbaud's poem and poetic theory: 'You devised some incoherent and heteroclite thoughts, from which a small, monstrous foetus is born, which you then put in a glass jar. . . . And be careful, with your theory of the seer, that you don't end up in the jar yourself, a monster in the museum.' Rimbaud's reply to his teacher's inevitable caution must have been violent and obscene, for Izambard was sufficiently miffed as to send it to Madame Rimbaud. Izambard may have been intending to clear himself of any possible intimations of homosexual conduct with Rimbaud, who may himself have set a rumour abroad, and thus wanted to come clean before the latter's mother. How better to vindicate himself than to point to Arthur's homo-erotic poetry and to the psychotic notions inherent in his poetic theory? One can imagine the storm at home; Rimbaud's hysteria, his nervous frustration, must have had him spring at his mother like a cornered rat. They were all trying to interfere with his mind. Those whose limitations extended to monotheism, provincialism, inveterately inherited moral values. What could Rimbaud with his Messianic quest have to do with this?

He continues:

This future will be materialistic, as you see. – Always full of *Number* and *Harmony*, these poems will be made to endure. – Essentially, it will be Greek Poetry again, in a way.

Eternal art will have its functions, since poets are citizens. Poetry will no longer lend rhythm to action; it *will be in advance*.

There will be poets like this! When the endless servitude of woman is broken, when she lives for and by herself, man – up till now abominable – having given her her freedom, she too will be a poet! Woman will discover the unknown! Will her world of ideas differ from ours? – She will discover strange things, unfathomable, repulsive and delicious; we shall accept them, we shall understand them.

Meanwhile, let us ask the *poet* for something *new* – ideas and forms. All the smart alecks will soon think they have satisfied this demand: – but it is not so.

The prophetic note inherent in Rimbaud's visionary prescriptions, which demand both a return to the intuitive response of primitive poetry and a means of projecting into the future – 'let us ask the *poet* for something *new*' – is a dramatic anticipation of certain modes of thought which have become a pattern in the twentieth century. Rimbaud had already dismissed his century as inert, immobile and little likely to improve. By mid-century poetry is usually stuck in a rut, and a plethora of derivative poets continue to live off the major voice from an earlier time. Like Lautréamont, Rimbaud was already living in the century he was never to reach. He would have poetry live in advance of action, rather than be the reflective principle commenting on the age's discoveries. It is up to the poet to get there first. 'And there will be poets like this!' he assures us. They were to come in number in another time, another place. Rilke, Trakl, Apollinaire, Breton, St-John Perse, Eliot, Neruda, Montale – these are a few who have brought a new poetics to bear on the twentieth century. And Rimbaud envisages the psychosexual emancipation of women. She too has a vital part to play in the discovery of the unknown. Once she has freed herself from man's 'abominable' denial and repression of her inner motives, she will more closely respond to the poetic summons than man, with his overriding impulse towards warfare and territorial imperatives.

Rimbaud was looking for a new race, a people who would invent the future according to the instruction of vision. The world could be imagined into existence. The atman, the suprahuman, was he who cultivated his visionary faculties for the arrival of a new dawn.

Rimbaud knew himself capable of undertaking the heroic task

he had set the poet, one even more daring in its social implications than Shelley's animated conviction that the imagination represents creative fire. Shelley's *Defence of Poetry* comes close to Rimbaud's Lettres du voyant in its declared Promethean beliefs that the inspired poet re-creates the world. Poets are in Shelley's words, 'the unacknowledged legislators of the universe'. But Shelley's upbringing, his classical education, his mythomania, would never have allowed him to go as far as Rimbaud. To conceive of the poet as 'the great criminal', and to suggest that women have as important a part to play in imaginative discovery as men, are ideas that link Rimbaud not only with the succeeding century but with ongoing continuity. There will never be a poetry in which Rimbaud does not play a part.

In reality he was too poor even to stamp his letters. His mother believed that if she deprived him of money he would either return to his studies or be forced to find a job. He consented to neither. If he was questioned, he replied: 'Shit'. He threw lice from his hair at Charleville antagonists, and gave readings of poems such as 'Accroupissements', 'Les Premières Communions' and 'Le Cœur volé' at Charles Bretagne's house. Someone had to be shot down. Banville was a good target; the florist poet whom Rimbaud had begun by tolerating was ripe to receive a satellite message of Rimbaudian insolence. Having satirized Banville in his poem 'Ce qu'on dit au poëte à propos de fleurs', he thought it necessary to remind the eminent poet of his existence.

Sir and dear Master
Do you remember receiving from the provinces, in June 1870, a hundred or a hundred and fifty mythological hexameters entitled *Credo in unam*? You were kind enough to answer!

The same imbecile is sending you the above verses, signed Alcide Bava. – I beg your pardon.

I am eighteen. – I shall always love Banville's verses.

Last year I was only seventeen!

Have I made any progress?

ALCIDE BAVA.
A.R.

41

Had Banville made any progress? By writing 'Le Bateau ivre', Rimbaud had not only given support to his poetic theory but at a stroke had liquidated his contemporaries. As if in preparation for another autumnal departure, he had written 'Le Bateau ivre' in August 1871. No matter the case put forward for the poem being influenced by Rimbaud's reading of such books as Michelet's *La Mer*, Jules Verne's *Vingt mille lieues sous les mers* (Twenty Thousand Leagues under the Sea), Poe's sea stories like *The Narrative of A. Gordon Pym* and *A Descent into the Maelstrom*, Baudelaire's *Le Voyage*, and whatever other fabulous accounts of the ocean he may have derived from literary sources, 'Le Bateau ivre' is more than all of these the undertaking of a great inner journey. Everything that had happened to this boy who was still not seventeen is compounded into the poem's violent and multi-coloured mosaic. It is the culmination of Rimbaud's childhood obsessions, and provides the metaphorical vessel for his flight not only from Charleville but from the visible world. We know biographically that as a child Rimbaud used to push a boat out into the green river Meuse, as far as its mooring-chain would permit, and that at home he would stretch out on a piece of canvas in his room, imagining sails, sea-roads, tropical islands, the spiritual freedom that comes with leaving the earth behind. And this poem, so fiercely innovative, so charged with visionary colour, was to be the credential with which he would face the Parnassians in Paris. Moreover, it was the poem he was to send to Paul Verlaine by way of an introduction to his inflammatory genius.

What was it like for Rimbaud in that intolerable August of 1871? He had written a poem so powerful, so far in advance of anything he had known or seen, a poem which remains one of the great works of imaginative lyricism; but he was no one outside his own estimate. The lapidary fire that blazes in the aqueous quatrains that make up 'Le Bateau ivre' had been living in his head for how long? He had no idea. It was enough that he could do it without inquiring into the poem's source. He ate little, he was growing physically, his clothes resembled a tramp's, there was no one with whom he could discuss the trauma attendant on being raped, and his obscenity was viciously scatological.

On occasions, Rimbaud would risk crossing the border into Belgium, a nine-mile walk through woods, in which a Customs officer might show up, demanding at gunpoint to know what Rimbaud and his friend Delahaye had concealed about their persons. What Rimbaud wanted from the grocery shops on the border was tobacco. And for him, this idea of breaking frontiers accorded with what he was doing on a mental plane in poetry. The journey to the border by way of La Grande Ville and Pussemange involved danger, but it was also an act of assertive rebellion. Rimbaud was stripping himself down. He was returning to the primitive. He would surprise the material world by coming at it naked. What he had inside was the imaginative equivalent of nuclear fission. What else was 'Le Bateau ivre' but the poetic equivalent of splitting the atom?

But Rimbaud, the child, needed help. In a second letter to Paul Demeny, dated 28 August 1871, he describes his mother 'as inflexible as seventy-three administrations with steel helmets'. The Ardennes are killing him. There is no relief for his inner turmoil. His mother insists that he takes a job in Charleville – and her Charleville and his are very different places. His, when he thinks of it, is a sun-bleached region. No matter how much he despises the narrowness of the people, it is nevertheless a region that has served as the physical backdrop to his poetry. Its limitations had provided the raw material for 'Le Bateau ivre'. Was it not the frustration of watching the lifeless meanderings of the Meuse which had set up the tension to create a sea, and more than that to imagine things that man has never seen? 'Et j'ai vu quelquefois ce que l'homme a cru voir!'

'This is the disgusting handkerchief which has been stuffed into my mouth,' Rimbaud imparted to Demeny in the same letter, referring to his sense of domestic and intellectual suffocation. The way out had to come. Rimbaud imagined that Paris was the right place for him to be, despite the ignominy he had suffered on his several visits there. Paris could not be worse than Charleville, although Rimbaud had not yet reckoned on genius being solitary by nature. At that moment in time, he would have been understood nowhere. When he finally scuttled to the desert, it was in the conscious realization that he would always be a pariah. And it is not an overstatement to claim that his mission was Messianic. He believed himself endowed with a prophetic message. He travelled in poverty on the roads between towns; he renounced all hope of material security. He is at the time, he tells Demeny, 'engaged in an infamous, inept, obstinate, mysterious work, answering questions, coarse and evil apostrophes with silence, appearing worthy in my extra-legal position'. But how could Rimbaud make known what he knew? In 'Le Bateau ivre' he had written:

> J'ai heurté, savez-vous, d'incroyables Florides
> Mêlant aux fleurs des yeux de panthères à peaux
> D'hommes! Des arcs-en-ciel tendus comme des brides
> Sous l'horizon des mers, à de glauques troupeaux!

> J'ai vu fermenter les marais énormes, nasses
> Où pourrit dans les joncs tout un Léviathan!
> Des écroulements d'eaux au milieu des bonaces,
> Et les lointains vers les gouffres cataractant!

> I have struck, you know, unbelievable Floridas
> and seen staring from flowers panthers' eyes
> in human skin. Rainbows stretched like bridles
> under the skyline to the green-grey herds!

> I have seen swamps stinking in fermentation,
> a Leviathan rotting in the reeds,
> water avalanching into a calm,
> distances cataracting blazing foam!

In 'Le Bateau ivre' Rimbaud had conceived a world into which he wished to escape. Escorted by sea-horses beneath ultramarine skies, pushing through violet fog towards the 'million gold birds', encountering green nights, delirium, electric moons, glaciers, brown gulfs, straining always towards the ineffable, he had been set free. He had created a universe: words had imploded into a self-generated cosmos. Nothing in 'Le Bateau ivre' could have existed without his having invented it. He had burnt a hole through the nineteenth century into the twentieth and the twenty-first. But he was still in Charleville.

His mind was huge with poetry. He could write it anywhere: on the *tabula rasa* of a cloud drifting across the countryside, on planes of water, on the earth, in his heart, on his mother's backside, anywhere he chose. Or it could go on paper; and it could be sent into the world. 'Le Bateau ivre', together with 'Mes petites amoureuses', 'Paris se repeuple', and 'Les Premières Communions', was dispatched to Verlaine, who in his reply hinted: 'I have something like a whiff of your lycanthropy.' This admission was like a signature written in blood. There was someone else out there who knew what it was like to leap for the throat. But Rimbaud still had to get there. He would risk everything and regret nothing. It was September. A gold light. A hint of change in the air. Too much adrenalin in his stomach. What if it all went wrong? He was staking his life on poetry. There was the Fontemps wood near Evigny to be visited with Delahaye for a last time. Rimbaud was naturally shy, apprehensive, awkward. Part of him knew that he would never find acceptance in the Paris salons. We know from Delahaye's book on Rimbaud that the latter read him 'Le Bateau ivre' on their last afternoon in the Evigny woods. Delahaye was overtaken to the point whereby he believed that 'There seemed to be no doubt that immediate success and fame in the near future awaited him.'

And Rimbaud? Beneath it all he was still a child, no matter his cool dissociation from emotion, and his contempt for all human relations. But there was the train. Paris represented madness. He would live out his delirium and burn.

Chapter Three

Rimbaud and Verlaine. So what? Much has been written about them, their intimate, antagonistic relationship documented by conjecture and partial evidence (unfortunately Verlaine's wife destroyed Rimbaud's letters to her husband), but what is important to the present book is delirium. The ramifications of the couple's emotional incompatibility, the impossibility of their living together and at the same time the terrible fear of separation that each entertained, helped whip Rimbaud's poetic impulse to a short, sustained frenzy. Rimbaud's desperation with life made him insensible to the reality of the relationship, and also helped condition the sadism in his nature, which was fed into Verlaine's nerves like a hot wire.

Whatever hopes of literary success Rimbaud may have nurtured before taking up life in Paris, were extinguished soon after his arrival there. He was shy and had cultivated arrogance as a defence; he was suited neither to obsequiousness nor hypocrisy, and who were these avuncular, socially acceptable men pretending to be poets? Rimbaud had arrived in order to set fire to the city. His mind burnt holes in paper, his images contained the primal hunger of big cats stalking prey in the jungle. What is more, he arrived in the city with lice in his hair, and an appearance so unkempt that it repelled those with whom he came into contact. At the time, Verlaine was without a proper income and was living with his seventeen-year-old wife, Mathilde Mauté de Fleurville, in her parents' house in the Rue Nicolet Montmartre. Right from the start, Rimbaud experienced hostility and condescension from Verlaine's wife and mother-in-law, and he withdrew. Vulnerable and hypersensitive, Rimbaud's instinct whenever he was made to feel socially inferior was to lock himself into a hedgehog's prickly ball and say nothing. Silence was his way of expressing disdain.

So this was Paris. Verlaine, the poet in whom he had expected to find a corresponding madness, was living a bourgeois life punctuated only on occasions by violent outbursts of drunkenness. Rimbaud was disillusioned. Why should he renounce his country ways? He used to lie at the entrance to the house, or in the drive, basking like a dog in the late summer sunlight. He didn't care that he had no change of clothes, no money, no future. He had vision. No one in that capital had conceived of a poem like 'Le Bateau ivre'. Lautréamont was already dead. He had died unknown after placing a black rainbow in the sky which would be seen and acknowledged by all future visionaries. Lautréamont had already risked more than Rimbaud was to take on; his extremes broke with everything, while Rimbaud proved reluctant to sever his poetry from Catholic symbolism. Rimbaud could have starved. Less than a year before his arrival in Paris, the Goncourts had noted in their journal that a servant in a food queue was there to buy for his restaurateur employer 'cats at six francs, rats at one franc, and dog-flesh at one franc fifty, the pound'. Rimbaud would probably have eaten rat with sadistic relish.

And far from showing deference to the Parnassians, Rimbaud outwardly manifested his contempt for their limitations. Coppée, Mendès, Heredia, Banville, Blémont, Valade – they had no purchase on Rimbaud's genius. They regarded him as satanic. 'Satan in the midst of the doctors' is how Léon Valade described Verlaine's young protégé with his blue eyes, red face and big hands and feet. They would gladly have seen the back of him, that upstart who wished to demolish their inveterate alexandrines. Nor had they any intention of publishing Rimbaud; he was quickly being consigned to the mental desert which in time was to become a physical reality.

A contributory factor to Rimbaud's psychological detachment from reality – he always lived on the outside – was the inherent cruelty in his nature, a side of him which was to feed mercilessly on Verlaine's indecisive character. Henri Mercier remembered seeing Rimbaud outside a theatre, concealed amongst the coach-horses, intently blowing smoke into one of the animal's nostrils. And this act was not intended as a joke; Rimbaud had singled out an animal in order to torment it maliciously. Later on he would do the same to Verlaine with a knife. Poetic commitment and the nervous charge generated by writing often create in poets the need for weird, unstabilizing compensations. Creative energy is rarely bivalent in its dualistic properties; it is nearly always ambivalent. The poet in receipt of inspiration may well react by attempting to subvert his gift. He may adopt a way of life that appears negative as a deliberate challenge to the source that involuntarily fuels his work.

Rimbaud quickly became an itinerant lodger, sleeping on floors, making do with whatever was offered him for a night, a week or a month. It was not until Verlaine paid for Rimbaud to have a room in the Rue Campagne Première that he occupied an independent address. It was here that he was able to pursue his belief in the systematic derangement of the senses, for he now lived in a permanent state of intoxication, either stoned on hashish or blind drunk on absinthe in the cafés of the Boul' Mich. Rimbaud called absinthe 'that sage of the glaciers', and his natural violence was undoubtedly exacerbated by excesses. Verlaine also became violent under the influence of absinthe; but his reasons for getting drunk were very different from those of Rimbaud, for Verlaine saw alcohol as an anaesthetic for his tortured sexuality, whereas for Rimbaud it was a stimulant to incite hallucinated vision. Verlaine would return home to Mathilde after a night's drinking and beat her black and blue. He split her lip, set fire to her hair, and was the more enraged by her passive behaviour, her pacific response to his emotional and physical savagery. Mathilde knew it was not Verlaine who was beating her, but Rimbaud. It was the mockery Rimbaud made of Verlaine's relationship, and the violence with which he contested it, that were projected into Verlaine's compacted fists, his obscene mouth. Rimbaud's derisive voice must have reverberated in his head.

Again, it was the element of sadism in Rimbaud that appeased itself by instigating Verlaine's domestic ruin. Young as he was, Rimbaud could discern Verlaine's weaknesses, and the sado-sexual furore at the centre of their relationship was exploited by Rimbaud as a means of further weakening his prey. It is doubtful that Rimbaud ever loved anyone; but at the time he needed Verlaine as a companion on the road, and as someone on whom he could vent his fury. Despite Verlaine's having made a small name for himself amongst his Parnassian contemporaries, Rimbaud had already overtaken his friend's achievements, and it was obvious to him that Verlaine lacked the inner credentials and mental ferocity needed to become a seer.

Something of the hysterical nature of Rimbaud and Verlaine's relationship at this time is recounted by Porché in 'Verlaine tel qu'il fut'. Porché tells us that, one evening at the Café du Rat Mort, Rimbaud asked Verlaine to place his hands flat on the table. When the latter had done so, Rimbaud pulled a knife from his pocket and quickly slashed Verlaine's hands. Not content with that, he followed Verlaine out into the street, and again set about him with the knife. The scandal of their relationship spread, and Rimbaud, who cultivated a propensity to shock, was gratified to see Verlaine's marital relations irretrievably ruined. And there is reason to believe that Rimbaud was too powerful at this time, and that there was an imbalance in his adept's oscillation between light and dark. The magician's attraction to the black art, to a concourse with evil and the authoritative power it generates, must have appealed to Rimbaud with his desire for overreach through sensory disturbance. It is unlikely that Rimbaud had the money, discipline or knowledge to prac- tise alchemy in the manner of following through the metallurgi- cal permutations from black to white, to yellow to red. His method was to raid books rather than read them. But there is every sign in his work of his being acquainted with the potency of alchemical symbols, and of having undertaken the alchemical mutations on a spiritual level. Rimbaud was searching for a state of madness which could be translated into poetry. Alchemical gold is contained within the black or, as it is termed, the nigredo. Rimbaud at this time of his life seems to have situated himself within alchemical black. And the sex he practised with Verlaine by way of the dark passage was another process towards ultimate mystic illumination. Rimbaud who advocated the abdication of the ego – 'Je est un autre' – pursued a schizoid search to inhabit a tenable double. And it is well known in magic that the imagination excited by sexual currents can be set to function at astral levels. It can work for the poet independent of him, and serves as a reservoir of radioactive energies. This emptying out, this voluntary letting go a hold on reality that the poet achieves in order to be in touch with inspirational forces, or for Rimbaud dementia, entertains the risk of possession by good or evil. It is a form of transference. The poet or adept is waiting for an energy build-up which he would not otherwise have been able to achieve. And when the current builds, the effect is one of shock. Rimbaud must have appeared devastating at such times, reified by an image, manic in his assertion of unmediated occult ambience. In his book *Cults of the Shadow*, Kenneth Grant tells us:

> Radio-active energies released by magicians using the Ophidian Current are so potent that when functioning to the full extent of their magical capacity few people can support their physical presence. Crowley's aura, for instance, was highly charged in this way; it inspired in some people a quite inexplicable dread. MacGregor Mathers described his encounter with High Adepts in terms suggesting similar conditions, and it is well known that Eliphaz [*sic*] Levi inspired panic-terror in the spirit-medium, D.D. Home.

It is this characteristic that must have been the root cause of Rimbaud's domination of Verlaine. He could paralyse the weaker man by an influx of energy. His Luciferian qualities were infallible. Verlaine's 'infernal bridegroom' (to use Rimbaud's term, *époux infernal*) was capable of slitting his jugular. In *Une saison en enfer* Rimbaud describes himself through Verlaine's imagined empathy:

> '. . . I belong to a distant race: my ancestors were Scandinavians: they used to slash their bodies, drink their own blood. –

I want to knife my body all over, tattoo it, I want to be as hideous as a Mongol: you will see, I shall howl in the streets. I want to become mad with rage. Don't show me jewels, for I shall crawl and writhe on the carpet. I want my wealth stained with blood. I shall never work. . . .' On several nights, his demon seized me, we rolled on the ground, I wrestled with him! – Often at night, drunk, he lay in wait in the streets, or in houses, to scare me to death. – 'They will really cut my throat; it will be disgusting.'

When Rimbaud wrote *Une saison en enfer*, it was as a valediction to poetry. But we can receive this passage as suggestive of the delirious state in which he lived out his visionary quest, and as a portrayal of the tempestuousness of his relationship with Verlaine. Although the latter believed absolutely in Rimbaud's untutored genius, he was at the time resentful that Rimbaud had interposed between him and his wife, and at times of grievance, when the couple lacked money, or were numbed by the cold in squalid London rooms, Verlaine's emotional scar must have opened. It is then they must have fought physically, Verlaine vehemently accusing Rimbaud of having ruined his life.

Rimbaud seems briefly to have generated the occult energy we associate with fascination. Levi and Crowley possessed it, and so too did Mick Jagger in the late sixties with his adoption of a Lucifer persona when performing songs like 'Sympathy with the Devil', 'The Midnight Rambler' and 'Gimme Shelter'. At the time of the murders and brutal maimings at the Rolling Stones' Altamont Freeway concert in December 1969, the Luciferian character that Jagger was able to project was something of which Rimbaud would have approved. For while the surrealists claimed Rimbaud as their precursor, so too must he be seen as the progenitor of the revolutionary youth who turned music into a social weapon in the sixties. Rimbaud, like Lautréamont, stands on the threshold of the cataclysmic changes which have dominated the twentieth century: the great wars, internal and external, the re-evaluation of the roles played by sex and religion, gender and work, the psychoanalytical interpretation of dream and the collective unconscious, all are anticipated by these two young poets whose vision apprehended a new universe. Rimbaud is always in the background of change. On the day the world ends, his face may well look out from billboards on the freeways. Arthur Rimbaud photographed by Carjat: reincarnated as X: now believed to be living in Beverly Hills. An indestructible survivor.

In the absence of Rimbaud's correspondence with Verlaine, the one reliable account of his life in Paris, and of the poetic vision to which he aspired, comes from a letter Rimbaud sent Ernest Delahaye in June 1872.

Now, it is at night that I work. From midnight to five in the morning. Last month, my room on Rue Monsieur-le-Prince looked out on a garden of the Lycée St Louis. There were enormous trees under my narrow window. At three in the morning, the candle went pale; all the birds cried at once in the trees: it is over. No more work. I had to look at the trees and the sky, fixated by that indescribable hour, the first in the morning. I could see the lycée dormitories, absolutely still. And already the jerky, sonorous, staccato noise of carts on the boulevards. I smoked my hammer-pipe, sitting on the tiles, for my room was a garret. At five o'clock I went downstairs to buy bread; it was the time. Workmen were up and about. For me, it was time to get drunk in the bars. I returned to my room to eat, and went to bed at seven in the morning, when the sun makes the wood-lice crawl out from under the tiles. What has always delighted me here is the early morning in summer and the December evenings.

We know this room was in the Hôtel de Cluny, Place de la Sorbonne. It was in that stifling hole that Rimbaud pursued his stages towards attaining poetic madness. He longed for the cool rivers of the Ardennes and for the countryside around Charleville. The torrid summer scorched him: he referred to Paris as Parshit. And how many times did he and Verlaine make love in that attic, soured by the reek of sweat, peppered by termites, foul with the acidic stench of urine rising from the courtyard. Rimbaud wanted everything and nothing. Absolute material power and starving asceticism. Neither would have made him happy. And at least in Verlaine he had a lover who understood the poverty attendant on being a poet. With his stinking body, ragged clothes and lack of money, Rimbaud could not have embarked on a relationship with anyone else even if he had tried.

Rimbaud's letter to Delahaye tells us things about Rimbaud which the latter may have been realizing for the first time when writing the letter. Very often you do not keep pace with what you are doing until you crystallize it through words. In this letter Rimbaud is in the process of recollecting himself. Drugs can take you so far out that you live independent of who you are. You can go on doing things without ever knowing that it is 'you' who are really involved. The journey back is one of dissociation. You have been sitting up five days and you thought it was only five hours. What a gain and what a waste!

For Rimbaud it was night. He was in passage. 'Maintenant, c'est la nuit que je travaince.' He is in crossing. The journey from dark to light is one of work. The adept celebrates the dawn only after his work has reached a temporary conclusion. In June the light comes at three. Rimbaud notices it only by the diminution of candlelight. He experiences the drug user's sense of too much light, the rush that burns. Suddenly the window is white. Birds are in confabulation. Day has broken on another reality. It is not his, but the drug wearing off means he is a part of it. There is nothing to do but smoke, listen to the dawn traffic and then go down to the street, half starved, strung out, looking first of all for the appeasement of wine, bewildered by the workaday world – the men already travelling across the city to their various jobs. The poet takes a baguette back to his room. What else can he afford? His pockets are in tatters.

We are privileged to have Rimbaud's intimate portrayal of a typical working night during his Paris stay. He seems to have acquired a drug dependency during the years 1872–3, for, when he returned to Roche in the spring of 1873 Paterne Berrichon, relying on information given to him by Rimbaud's sister Isabelle, tells us that his skin was grey, his pupils contracted, his body suffering from malnutrition. He would lie on his bed for hours, shut up in the dark, raving. The 'Mauvais sang' from *Une saison en enfer*, was his own bad blood, the cells craving for narcotics. What he took was hashish and opium; he may well have had access to morphine. He must have stolen to get the money to score.

When Rimbaud left Paris in July 1872, a month after writing to Delahaye about his nocturnal life there, it was without his having achieved the literary fame that he had thought so easily within his reach. The next six months were to be a time of psychic and physical upheaval. With Verlaine he visited Brussels, and in September of that year the two of them took up residence in London. And it was probably there that he wrote most of the experimental prose poems that have come down to us as *Les Illuminations*. Both he and Verlaine were deeply disturbed, and no matter the consolation that their relationship appeared to afford, the combined leakage of Verlaine's self-pity and Rimbaud's resolution to derange himself in the interests of poetry must have created a negative charge inimical to every hope of a positive future together. Dependent on Verlaine's mother for money and whatever little they could earn by teaching French to English students, their lives appeared to be mutilated by an irreversible poverty. And Rimbaud had hoped for so much from poetry. While Verlaine was preparing his collection *Les Romances sans paroles* for his publisher Lepelletier, Rimbaud undertook his work without the incentive of publication. His writing was directed towards no public; its dynamic anticipated a still unrealized future. Part of Rimbaud's impetuosity, his impatience with poetry as a form capable of containing his imaginative volatility, is reflected in his self-destructive behaviour at this time. He had overtaken himself; poetry was and still is trying to keep track with his fearless assault on the imaginal *sanctum regnum*.

'Peut-on s'extasier dans la destruction, se rajeunir par la cruauté!' ('Can man reach ecstasy through destruction and be rejuvenated by cruelty?') Rimbaud's 'Conte' in *Les Illuminations* poses the question relevant to his own emotional battlefield at the time of his shared life with Verlaine. Something of Rimbaud's state of delirium, induced by drugs and poetic tension, sounds like a drumbeat through these elliptical and often hermetic allegories in which his imagery crystallizes to a lapidary brilliance around physical shifts of landscape which impart to the reader the sensation of looking out of an aircraft window at the visible changes of terrain.

Throughout *Les Illuminations* Rimbaud uses hallucination as a means of seeing. And maintaining that pitch, whereby the psyche introjects sensory experience before it can be rationalized by interpretation through the external world, imposes an inflammable strain on the nerves. Its demands are those made on the dervish, and one suspects that Rimbaud would have found an exalting influence in the thirteenth-century Persian mystic poet, Rûmî, had his works been known to him. The transcendent vision that Rûmî cultivated was one in which the barrier between man and God was extinguished. Rûmî's mystical illuminations find a correspondence with Rimbaud's: both are poets intent on achieving a vision of truth through sensory intoxication.

In 'Conte' Rimbaud tells us that the Prince, who adopts Rimbaud's sadistic persona, 'amused himself by cutting the throats of rare animals. He set palaces on fire. He fell on people and hacked them to pieces. – The crowd, golden roofs and the beautiful creatures continued to exist'. In this passage Rimbaud accentuates the contradiction at the heart of poetry. What takes place as an imaginative reality activated by the poet's nervous charge and directed towards a homicidal destruction is neutralized by extraneous evidence. The poet's world is one of dualities. The transformations he causes to take place happen somewhere else; and nor is action on the inner plane parallel to that which happens on a temporal dimension. Poetry anticipates the future, but there is a time-lag. Things happen too quickly and too radically in terms of inner space. The poet can create or annihilate within that context; but in his lifetime he may not see his vision realized. Psychic travel moves at the speed of light and eliminates logical connections. The arc pursued by the poem is meteoric; it burns off excess in flight and earths itself in a place where it will be discovered at the right time.

Les Illuminations is full of references to the alchemical work; the transformation of the ego into the sublimated psyche. 'Métropolitain' concludes with an affirmation of the mystic's power. 'In the morning when, with Her, you fought in the dazzle of snow, the green lips, the ice, the black flags and blue rays, and the purple perfumes of the polar sun – your strength.' The experience described here is analogous to that encountered in Rimbaud's alchemical night 'Matinée d'ivresse'. 'We have been promised that the tree of good and evil will be buried in darkness, that tyrannical honesty will be exiled, so that we may flourish in our pure love. It began with feelings of disgust and it ends – since we could not seize eternity immediately – with a riot of perfumes.'

Rimbaud's demand is one of immediate knowledge; his aesthetic doctrine approved of dynamic change. In his discourse with the work he had been promised that a new love would replace 'the tree of good and evil', and within the poem it had. Part of Rimbaud's disappointment with poetry can be attributed to the time-lag he felt disrupted the action of conceiving the poem, and the failure of that vision to make good in the socio-economic ethos in which the poet lived. Rimbaud's battle is fought within this tension field. He uses delirium to counteract temporal inertia. His poetic world is one of heightened colour, magnified sensory stimuli, a universe in which the imagination is sovereign. He constantly resembles someone who paints in a dream, and on awakening is distraught to find that the world is unaltered by his private action. He runs out into the street searching for his violet skies, black ice, green clouds, only to find a washed-out blue sky tenting the city, the ordinary day going on with its uneventful people. And by way of retaliation, the poet only further intensifies his intrinsic findings. He creates in order to contravene the natural order of things, the poem working in dialectical opposition to reality. Rimbaud's genius is inseparable from attack. Failing to find the world altered by his vision, he sets about deconstructing the latter. There are times when Rimbaud reminds me of Jackson Pollock, whose drunkenness and physicality in his handling of paint demanded a brutal confrontation with his canvas.

During the autumn and early winter of 1872 Rimbaud and Verlaine struggled to survive in London. Verlaine was besieged by blue court papers dealing with his wife's justifiable demands for separation and a claim for yearly maintenance of twelve hundred francs. But the undertones were worse. Mathilde had been advised to bring court accusations of homosexuality against her husband, an offence which at the time involved not only literary and social ruin but could also carry with it a prison sentence. Moreover, Rimbaud was still a minor. Verlaine could be accused not only of abduction but illegal sex: in a word, paedophilia.

In the poem 'Vagabonds' in *Les Illuminations* Rimbaud expresses an irritated compassion for his maudlin, intoxicated friend. Rimbaud had clearly outgrown the relationship; poetry had failed them both in terms of its providing for them in the material world. Rimbaud's dream of discovering a universal panacea through his studies as a mage had resulted in acute poverty. His boots leaked, he slept in his clothes for additional warmth, and whatever money came to him he immediately spent on liquor and drugs.

Poor brother! What terrible nights I owed him! 'I had no deep feeling for the affair. I played on his weakness. Through my fault, we would return to exile and slavery.' He believed I had a weird form of bad luck and innocence, and he added disquieting reasons.

I would reply by jeering at this satanic doctor, and would end by leaving through the window. I created, along the countryside streaked with bands of rare music, mirages of a future night parade.

After that vaguely hygienic distraction, I would stretch out on a straw mattress. And, almost every night, as soon as I was asleep, my poor brother would get up, his mouth dry and his eyes protruding – just as he dreamt himself to be – and would drag me into the room howling his deranged dream.

One can accept this as dictated by the mood in which Rimbaud wrote, with all the fluctuating contradictions and immediate impulsion this entails, but for all that there is an authenticity here, if not honesty, and one feels that this is how it was. Their nights must have been terrible. One can imagine Rimbaud frozen into a mood of defiant and intractable hostility likely to enrage a man who is seeking consolation for his distraught emotions. And what is more, Rimbaud probably increasingly denied Verlaine sex ('I had no deep feeling for the affair'), thereby severing the one form of communication that might have led to a temporary reconciliation of hostility. Verlaine wanted both his wife and Rimbaud, and as the latter had been instrumental in insisting that he break with his wife, so Verlaine saw the vacuum open in which he anticipated himself alone. To the recipient, experiencing derision in the face of emotional suffering is comparable to having needles prodded into a wound. Verlaine must have accused Rimbaud of being satanic, of having invoked evil into their lives: his mouth must have been raw and monotonously obscene. And to accentuate Verlaine's fury, Rimbaud would exit by way of an open window, leaving his friend with the additional fear that he might not return. But for Rimbaud this temporary escape has an almost hallucinogenic quality. The 'countryside' in the city is 'streaked with bands of rare music' – he is somewhere else just by placing himself there in his head. For Rimbaud it is always the future that is important, what he sees are 'mirages of a future night parade'. His leap through the window is a projection into another time.

And to what did he return? Smashed glass on the floor. Verlaine's ugly imprecations, the sexual pleading of a dipsomaniac. Rimbaud was too strong to sink to this sort of thing. His excesses were taken as part of a poetic experiment, but he kept in control. He was always bigger than it, whereas for Verlaine absinthe was like a glacial pyramid around which his diminutive figure wandered, all the time decreasing in stature.

During this time Rimbaud may well have visited the Chinese opium dens by the river. His fascination for ships was not unlike that of Hart Crane's, and both men looked on the sea and sailors as a source affording access to ineffable mysteries. Crane's 'The seal's wide spindrift gaze towards paradise' belongs to the same thalassic mythology as Rimbaud's 'And at times ineffable winds would lend me their wings' from 'Le Bateau ivre'. Both poets conceived of poetry as inextricably linked with the out there – the expansive skyline.

It is possible that Rimbaud formed connections with sailors and dockers at this time – the cosmopolitan nature of the docks with their multifarious commerce was likely to stimulate his desire for travel. Rimbaud's great sea voyage had been undertaken as an imaginative journey; now he could see the big ships put in, smell the salt on their hawsers, watch the excitement of men come ashore from all quarters of the globe. There was commerce, profiteering, and there were drugs, animals, exotic cargoes, squalor, slavery, sexual liberties. Rimbaud was fascinated by this other world, which seemed to combine action with dream, voyage with contemplation. When he writes of the sea it is with the verbal opulence that St-John Perse was later to adopt in his extravagant oceanic mosaic, *Amers*.

Ladies strolling on terraces by the sea; children and giants, magnificent blacks in the green-grey moss, jewels standing on the rich soil of groves and thawed gardens – young mothers and older sisters whose eyes are full of pilgrimages, sultanas, princesses whose walk and clothes are tyrannical, foreign girls and those who are serenely unhappy. ('Enfance', *Les Illuminations*)

It is noticeable how one perception follows another, not so much as a stream of consciousness but as a collision whereby the friction generated by an image corresponds to an immediate visual successor. The feeling of disorientation that one undergoes in reading *Les Illuminations* is not dissimilar to the surprise connections made when one is spaced out on drugs. Things happen a long way away, and then surprise one by coming up close. Disjunction and conjugation of visual images are under such an accidental state. You can be preoccupied with a crack in the ceiling which expands to a seismic flaw with houses tilting lopsidedly above a valley – it is there and it is real – before the importance of a matchbox or table item takes over. The poetic image marries the earthquake and the matchbox. And it happened when? A minute, an hour or a year ago? There is no time for the user until the metabolism alerts the body to the insistence of renewing its need.

What did Rimbaud do in his London days? Verlaine's letters tell us that the two spent a lot of time walking around the city, drinking in the inhospitable bars, but expression of external events has little to do with time. It is a way of saying something happened today that makes me locatable to others. Rimbaud was secret and versatile. It is said that he worked on a street-stall in Paris on one of his first visits to the city. It is possible that he lived a double life and in doing so deceived Verlaine. He needed money to maintain his state of intoxicated vigil, and when you are that far up, and often not functioning, money has to be got fast and often inexpediently. Theft and prostitution are ways of cutting corners to raise immediate money. And Rimbaud, who had embarked on a ruthless system of psychophysical experimentation, would have viewed both exigencies as further means towards provoking the derangement he saw as necessary to truth. Verlaine was too drunk, too preoccupied with his etiolated marital affairs to be concerned with real time. The latitude granted to Rimbaud is a biographer's fiction; he was there, he was anywhere.

You are still at the temptation of Anthony. The struggle with diminished impetus, faces of a child's insolence, collapse and terror. But you will begin this work: all harmonic and architectural possibilities will rise up about your seat. Perfect, unlooked for creatures will offer themselves for your experiments. The curiosity of forgotten crowds and idle luxuries will circle dreamily around you. Your memory and your senses will serve to feed your creative impulse. What will become of the world, when you leave it? At all events, nothing of present aspects.   ('Jeunesse')

Something of Rimbaud's youthful desperation is expressed here. His vision was unique. How much time did he have? No one else could create the architectonics of his imagined cities and, as he saw it, no one else could save the world. His responsibility was to re-create the universe through the imagination. Most poets repeat endlessly their descriptions of an inherited world: their poems are about the actually attainable here and now. Rimbaud began by disinheriting all preconceptions. Only after renouncing the temporal world could he set about constructing a poetic future. To do this he had commerce with the past and present. 'Après le déluge' is a magnificent conjugation of myth and reconstructed history.

As soon as the idea of the Flood had subsided, a hare stopped in the clover and the undulating flower bells, and said its prayer through the spider's web to the rainbow.

Oh! the precious stones were hiding – already the flowers looked about them.

In the dirty high street stalls were set up, and boats were hauled down to the sea, piled high as in old prints.

Blood flowed in Bluebeard's Castle – in the slaughterhouses – in the circuses, where God's seal whitened the windows. Blood flowed, and milk.

Beavers built. Coffee beakers smoked in the bars.
In the big house, its windows still dripping, children in mourning looked at marvellous pictures.

A door slammed, and, on the village square, a child waved his arms, and was understood by weathervanes and steeplecocks everywhere, under the abrupt shower.

Madame X installed a piano in the Alps. Mass and first communions were celebrated at the hundred thousand altars of the cathedral.

Caravans set out. And the Hôtel Splendide was built in the chaos of ice and polar night.

Since then, the moon has heard jackals howling across thyme deserts, and eclogues in wooden shoes growling in the orchard. Then, in the violet budding grove, Eucharis told me it was spring.

Rise, pond; – foam, pour over the bridge and over the woods; – black drapes and organ music – lightning and thunder, climb up in torrents; – waters and sorrows, rise and induce the Floods.

For since they vanished – oh! the burrowing jewels and the open flowers – we have been bored! and the Queen, the Witch who lights her fire in a clay pot, will never tell us what she knows and what we shall never know.

What Rimbaud creates in the best of *Les Illuminations* is a microcosm, a microstructured novel which depends for its success on dissociated sense connections. Periods of history alternate with immediate sensations in a way that had never been used before in poetry. Rimbaud is not interested in isolating a poetic theme and writing a poem around a subject, rather his poetry moves with the speed of thought. Our inner dialogue is interrupted by apprehending the external world. Rimbaud builds a poetry that advances like a shoal of fish which fans out around an obstruction and then resumes its nervous course. The power of the poet is such that he can suspend history. It is 'the idea of the Flood' which subsides rather than the deluge, and that event eliminated, the real happening can take place in inner space. The hare says its prayer 'through the spider's web to the rainbow'. It is the hare's dynamic action which creates a new world and makes the old story of the flood seem tame by comparison. Everything in Rimbaud's poetry is energized; inertia is his enemy. Things happen fast: 'Blood flowed', 'Beavers built', 'A door slammed', 'Caravans set out'. Novellas are suggested by single lines: 'Madame X installed a piano in the Alps.' And what of 'the Hôtel Splendide' which was built 'in the chaos of ice and polar night'?

Part of Rimbaud's frustration, which manifests itself to the full in *Une saison en enfer*, is brought about by the realization that poetry always withholds the irresolvable. The field set up by a poem is a diversification rather than a narrowing of focus. One metaphor creates another. The poet's despair is that these outriders set up alternative truths which in turn deflect from the poet's original aim. Rimbaud's fist cracks open to release diamonds, rubies, emeralds. They scatter and lodge where their individual trajectories cease. The images become incrustations; minerals in schist. And what does the poet do? Piss in the street. Imagine that everything will come all right in the end. Space out on drugs because the dream moves at a speed which is irreversible. Or sit there waiting? Waiting for the vision to replace reality, so that the jump out of the window is into the landscape of the poem.

Rimbaud, for all his tenacious independence and rebellion against domestic strictures, needed Verlaine as security. Because much of his correspondence was destroyed, we do not know a great deal about Rimbaud's private response to the life he was living in London. We can only piece it together from his poems, and poetry obeys a truth quite different from that of the life which conceives it. All we know is that by the beginning of December 1872 change was imminent. Verlaine wrote to Lepelletier: 'This week, Rimbaud must go back to Charleville and my mother is coming here.'

Verlaine faced personal ruin in France. The accusations of homosexuality were sufficient to ruin his literary career. He remained the victim of an insoluble dilemma. Part of him desired a reconciliation with his wife, while the rebel in him delighted in the notoriety that came of his relationship with Rimbaud. Still another part of him gravitated towards alcoholic dissolution and the dormant solitude attendant on heavy, unsociable drinking.

It must all have seemed unreal. So much had happened to Rimbaud in so short a time. He had abandoned his studies, renounced his home, offended the literati in Paris, lived through long nights of alchemical vigilance, experienced a ferocious relationship with an older, married man. He had tramped across roads, starved and fetched up in a foreign city. He had remained true to his belief that the visionary poet must disintegrate in order to reintegrate as the alchemical conjunctio. His hands were most likely caked with dirt. He had no change of clothes. What he ate he stole – milk bottles from doorways, fruit from street-barrows; but he could always afford bread. He had used his body as a biochemical experiment for drugs. He had written a poetry so far in advance of his contemporaries, he was already willing to accept that it was unpublishable. His papers and manuscripts were in custody, and Verlaine's wife and parents-in-law had no intention of letting them go. He was only just eighteen. What did life want of him and he of it? Poetry had in part failed him. He had expected to see in the external world some of the changes realized in his poetry. Why was everything so painfully slow? The poetic line was fast, immediate. In his poetry he had sent out assassins into the world. 'Voici le temps des ASSASSINS.' And in the same poem, 'Matinée d'ivresse', he had written: 'Nous avons foi au poison. Nous savons donner notre vie tout entière tous les jours.' ('We believe in poison. We know how to give all of ourselves every day.') These lines are a long way from the inspired sentiments of youth. This is the conviction of someone willing to risk 'poison' or hallucinogenes in the interests of higher truth. And the words of someone who knew how to give himself completely to his art, and to expend that sacrifice each day.

Blood on the wall, enamel from a chipped tooth. – It is Verlaine's.

A blue bruise spreading beneath the eye. – It is Rimbaud's.

A glass smashed on the floor. – It is anyone's.

Paper crackled into a ball and singed. – It is Rimbaud's.

An addressed envelope shredded. – It is Verlaine's.

The half-eaten baguette. – It is stolen.

The anger padding like thunder. – It is both of them.

The hysterical shriek. – It is Verlaine's.

The stolen money on the bed. – It is Rimbaud's.

The delirious scene in the mirror. – It is both of them.

And a fist banging on the door. – It is the police.

Let us invent a little story. It is late November 1872. Most biographers agree that Rimbaud returned to Charleville in December and went back to London in January 1873, after receiving a suicidal letter from Verlaine, who claimed to be desperately ill and dying of 'grief, sickness, boredom, desertion'. Rimbaud knew Verlaine to be lachrymose, moribund and stupefied by liquor. We do not know if Rimbaud embarked on writing *Une saison en enfer* immediately on his return to Charleville. It seems more likely that he worked on it during his Easter stay and again in the incandescent months – July and August. In my story Rimbaud visited the underground on his way back to Charleville. He was travelling light, as always. Books and paper stuffed into his misshapen coat, his drugged eyes looking for signs in the milling crowd. Who were they, the endless stream of faces pouring up the stairs and into the street? And why was he here and who was he at this moment in time? The prospect of returning home – Charleville was still occupied by the Prussians – brought the same sense of unrelieved despondency as did the idea of continuing with Verlaine in London. He had exchanged his mother's draconian rancour for the drunken, sadistic threats of a man whom he had come increasingly to disrespect. And what was worse, he had realized Verlaine's poetic limitations. This man would never become a seer. He did not even have the courage to drink the blood from his wounds as Rimbaud did. And, anyhow, the police were on to them, not only for Verlaine's activities with the Communards but for the apparent nature of their relationship.

Rimbaud lingered in the corridor before descending into the black pit beneath London. He was cold. His boots had taken in water. He was hungry. Ravaged by drugs, he had gone for days without being aware of the necessity to eat. His money permitted nothing more than his train and ferry. Now that the hash had worn off, he would eat anything. His fingers, his toes. There were tramps begging at the entrance to the station. He was poorer than they. Who cared for his light, his inestimable inner riches? And he was by this time no stranger to derelicts. He had slept out often enough to know their camaraderie in the countryside. They were men who had fallen through a hole in their lives and had no intention of returning to the society that had disowned them.

As Rimbaud lingered, a well-dressed man in a cashmere topcoat brushed against him. The man's reaction was one of disdain. It was as though he felt that the slightest contact with the poor carried with it disease. Rimbaud cursed the man in French. 'Merde! Cochon!' He would like to have run after him and thrown lice at the man's collar. What did they know, these arrogant, bellicose men whose machinations bled the natives all over the world under the euphemism of Empire? Indigenous cultures were eradicated in the name of their sanctimonious monotheism. Rimbaud spat.

There was someone who kept moving into his orbit – now here, now there, now gone again. Rimbaud had seen his face once. He was not sure if it was a Negro boy or girl; the person had dyed his hair blond to accentuate his mulatto features. Had he not encountered this young man at the docks? But he could not get off with him, as Verlaine was in a menacing mood. And the attraction was not sexual. It was something else. This man was the embodiment of his dream of the androgyne. And again he was something else. He represented a twisted beauty. It was as though he knew all things without ever having experienced them. He had seen oceans, white coves, foreign ports, places where he had gone ashore without knowing their geographical names. The scent of lemons, mangoes, the gulf breaking into flower; he had been to those countries that Rimbaud had visited in poems. His mouth was sensual, his hands bony. He too lived on the outside of life. There was no place for him in the centre; he had to keep to edges.

He was just standing there, his mouth open on nothing. He could not even articulate his need. Rimbaud kept thinking he had hallucinated the man into being. He was floating rather than standing with his back to the wall, an empty palm extended into the air.

When he went up to the image, it was real. The boy's hand tightened over his wrist. And then the light was coming at them as they went back up the stairs to the street – the cold, blue December light with its industrial reek. This slim young man led him quickly through alleys, through a blue door into a yard and up a flight of rickety stairs. He admitted them into a single room. It was bare. There was no heating, only a mattress on the floor, a huddle of blankets, a green macaw standing on a perch. There was a hookah on the floor, and the room smelt acrid.

They stood there shivering. There was light in this man. Rimbaud could feel its radial points in his hands, in his eyes. The Negro said: 'I know who you are.' And Rimbaud replied: 'I know who you are.' The sound of the street filled in their silence.

'Livre nègre' flashed up in Rimbaud's mind. It was a confirmation. All of his anger, his compassion, his conflicting sexuality, his poverty came to the surface. This stranger had sprung the book on him. It would be his valediction to poetry, and also his celebration of its dynamic. Life would never come right. Poetry in the end was always expendable, no matter that it operated as an undercurrent which changed the world. Rimbaud was ill and tired. He had found this one person who recognized his identity. He had no more than an hour to express his vision of the future, and this time words were not necessary. He could still make his train connection to the ferry. Light hardly filtered through the closed curtains. Both of them wanted it like that.

Chapter Four

The year 1873 was to prove the most intensive, cataclysmic and combustively creative period of Rimbaud's short-lived allegiance to poetry. It was a time of drug addiction and unsupervised withdrawal, a time of the irreparable fragmentation of his relationship with Verlaine, a time of brief hope that *Une saison en enfer* would explode across the literary scene, and as we know it, a time of disillusionment with poetry and an abandonment of his programme to derange his senses systematically.

Baudelaire called it 'le guignon' – bad luck, a leakage into the system which irreversibly poisons. Something had got into Rimbaud. The overwrought attunement of his nerves, sensitized to make of sensation a heightened reading of the world, was slackening their tension. He must often have been at breaking-point, but pride prevented him from saying so. Self-laceration was so deeply ingrained in him that he internalized pain as still another stage towards visionary experience. And he was facing the addict's continuous crisis; not only how to get the money to pay for drugs, but where to get the stuff. He must have taken a supply with him from London, and using up that quantity of opium and hashish may well have precipitated his sudden return to the capital on 12 January, far more so than Verlaine's lachrymose threat that he would kill himself if he continued his solitary suffering in London. Verlaine's mother may have taken her son seriously, but Rimbaud had experienced sufficient of his friend's emotional crises to know that this was simply another false alarm. But with the fifty francs sent him by Verlaine's mother, another escape from the constrictions of Charleville became possible.

Pierre Petitfils, in his biography *Rimbaud*, has drawn our attention to how both men were shadowed by the police in London, their political beliefs being as suspect as the nature of their relationship. On 26 June 1873, a note was transmitted to the Paris police prefecture which read: 'A liaison of a strange kind links the former employee of the Prefecture of the Seine (who remained at his post during the Commune), sometime poet on the Rappel, a M. Verlaine, and a young man who often comes to Charleville, and who, under the Commune, was a member of the Paris francs-tireurs, young Raimbault [*sic*]. M. Verlaine's family is so sure of the authenticity of this degrading fact that they are basing part of their case for a separation on this point.'

Of course they could not even get Rimbaud's name right, but the certainty that he and Verlaine were living together in a homosexual liaison carries a distinctly sinister undercurrent. Given that another police report, dated 1 August 1873, states that 'These two individuals fought and tore at one another like wild beasts, just for the pleasure of making it up afterwards', it is surprising that they were never investigated and arrested. Other occupants of the houses in Howland Street and Royal College Street must have overheard their violent physical quarrels and likewise their love-making. That their relationship evaded prosecution is peculiar in itself, and even when Verlaine was eventually sentenced for shooting Rimbaud through the wrist, there was no attempt to establish a prosecution case on the charge of sodomy. Verlaine was examined by the Belgian police and considered to have been involved in both active and passive sodomy just prior to his arrest; but the case did not pivot on this suppositional incriminating evidence.

In the period between January and April 1873, before Rimbaud returned to Charleville, he must have continued with the writing of *Les Illuminations*. In 'Enfance' he writes with the disorientation that comes of poetic delirium conflicting with the metabolic fluctuations contingent on drugs. The resultant clash and intermittent symbiosis give rise to an imagery that ignites with the combustion of petroleum. The poet's room becomes a subterranean gallery. A basement is a hypogeum and finally a room in space – the idea of a room.

Let them rent me this tomb, whitewashed with lines of cement in relief – deep underground.

I lean my elbows on the table, the lamp throws a bright light on newspapers and absurd books which I am foolish enough to reread.

At an enormous distance above my subterranean room, houses grow like plants, and fogs gather. The mud is red or black. Monstrous city, endless night!

Not so high up are the sewers. At my side, the breadth of the globe. Perhaps azure pits, wells of fire. It is perhaps at these levels moons and comets, seas and fables meet.

In my depressed hours, I imagine sapphire and metal balls. I am master of silence. Why should the appearance of an aperture turn pale at the corner of the ceiling?

Poetry, when its direction is flighted, when the connections made succeed by the logic of dissociation, rather than through the need to qualify individual constituents by reason, is a force that excites one's expectation of contact with the marvellous. Rimbaud suggests a universe on each outgoing breath. In his mind he is in a whitewashed, subterranean room. What is that room really like? You cannot get into someone's head to find that out, and he can tell you only by means of the visual image. The narrator here anticipates existential absurdity. Newspapers and meaningless books kill time; they are a sedative against what man fears most – the unlimited duration of the future. Above him is the red and black mud of the city, but before he can reach the surface there are the substrata of the imagination to be encountered. Inner space informs the poet of azure pits and flaming wells. Everything is possible there – 'moons and comets, seas and fables meet'. There is a compensation to be derived from creative depression, in that it often has the imagination realize an alternative world. Rimbaud imagines new planets, 'sapphire and metal balls'. And given the freedom of inner space, he is paranoid about external intrusions. What is going on out there while the poet is concentrated upon himself? Even the smallest thing takes on menacing proportions. 'Why should the appearance of an aperture turn pale at the corner of the ceiling?' When you are on drugs, any random detail that arrests the attention may be magnified into an event of universal significance. *Les Illuminations* is full of these intimations of paranoid stress. The drug is one state of unreality, the poem another, so that at a double remove from externals vulnerability is heightened. The genius of Rimbaud for creating worlds carries with it the corresponding disappointment that he has invented a paper bird rather than one which is going to fly. Ink is absorbed by paper, no matter the imaginative reach of thought. But all the same he challenges those on the outside: 'Qu'est mon néant, auprès de la stupeur qui vous attend?' ('What is my void compared with the stupefaction awaiting you?') And who would presume to take up that challenge?

In 'Vies' from *Les Illuminations* Rimbaud exemplifies the characteristics of the omnipotent mage. His claims are similar to those which he was to recount in retrospect in *Une saison en enfer*. Having told us 'A flight of scarlet pigeons thunders across my thoughts', he proceeds to magnify his attributes. His writing vindicates his youth – how else could he know so much other than by the acquisition of power through the imagination?

In a loft in which I was shut up when I was twelve, I understood the world, I illustrated the human comedy. In a cellar I learnt history. At a night celebration in a northern city I met all the wives of old painters. In a Paris alley I was taught the classical sciences. In a magnificent building surrounded by the Orient, I finished my huge work and spent my celebrated retirement. I set fire to my blood. I am released from my duty. I must give up all thought of it. I really am from beyond the grave, and without work.

The unorthodox manner of achieving knowledge and vision is one calculated to enrage pragmatists. Rimbaud had found in the imagination a faculty that undercut intellectual conventions. Moreover, he speaks as one who is reincarnated – he can remember finishing his immense work in the Orient. The building in which he lived suggests that he was rich then, and poor now. What he gained in another incarnation must be carried on at great suffering to the poet. The gifts carried forward are part of an invisible heritage. They are activated by memory: and recall is one of the chief constituents of the imaginative process.

In *Les Illuminations* Rimbaud is all the time telescoping vision into possible fictions that reduce the universe to something containable. Because the imagination is inexhaustibly expansive, the poet has in some way to shoot it down like a low-flying aircraft. And in the process he shoots himself down. He is the blackened survivor who finds himself on a beach at the end of the world. But the place is one he has imagined. There might be a single white villa cut into the cliff; a gold lion standing on the headland, a woman with a swathe of blonde hair playing the piano at the water's edge. Where is that? For the poet it is a place called home. And it is located in a habitable inner space.

Rimbaud gets to the lost country in so many ways. Sometimes it is situated beneath a lake or in the sky, or it becomes specific by reduction. And it is always the visual quality of his work which allows the imaginative to be located in the physical.

When the world has been reduced to a single dark wood for our dazzled eyes – to a beach for two faithful children – to a musical house for our clear understanding – I shall find you.

When there is only a single old man left on earth, serene and beautiful, living in unimaginable luxury – I shall be at your feet.

When I have realized all your memories, when I am the girl who can bind your hands – I shall suffocate you.   ('Phrases', op. cit.)

What Rimbaud possesses is the film-maker's art. In order to focus on the image, he reduces the world to what can be contained within the poetic lens. There is nothing else for viewing but 'a single dark wood', a still that excludes all other detail. And the sequence follows on in a series of frames: 'a beach for two faithful children' and then 'a musical house for our clear understanding'. One: two: three. Each image creates a consecutive microcosm. You can get there in the imagination by easy jumps; and this is how good poetry functions. When the visual landscape becomes peopled, it is with a clearly identified solitary – 'a single old man' – who is the sole occupant of Rimbaud's metaphoric planet. And part of his own insecurity, his search for a father-figure, is evident in his supplication to this man of unimaginable wealth. But having achieved the realization of sharing this last man's memories, Rimbaud by an abrupt mutation of gender becomes the girl who binds the man's hands and suffocates him.

Rimbaud and Verlaine. Verlaine and Rimbaud. What was happening to them? London and the British Museum; the attempt to learn English sufficient for them to teach French to private pupils. Always the need to keep on top of things so as to conceal their respective imbalances. With that in mind, Verlaine wrote to Emile Blémont:

> . . .We are learning English accordingly, Rimbaud and I, in Edgar Poe, in collections of popular songs, in Robertson, etc. etc. And also in shops, bars, libraries. We are gluing up our mouths to aid our pronunciation. Most days we go for long walks into the suburbs and countryside, Kew, Woolwich, etc., for we are familiar with London now. Drury Lane, Whitechapel, Pimlico, Angel, the City and Hyde Park, no longer hold the attraction of the unknown.

By April, both men had left London. Verlaine, who was still in a state of equivocal emotional turmoil over his wife, went off to stay with an aunt at Jehonville in Belgium. Rimbaud, who was without money and sufficient English for him to remain by himself in London, departed to join his family in Roche. It was still another return in a pattern that did not allow for alternatives. Boredom, a flatland, the iron stove of a mother, a farm at Roche worn to a state of disrepair, and above all the huge isolation, all of these things provided the negative charge that Rimbaud countered by writing *Une saison en enfer*. He arrived at Roche on Good Friday, 11 April. He brought with him no credentials. He had no book to show, no security in life, his relationship had been with a man and so could not be talked about; he was once again penniless. Regarded by his family as a degenerate urchin, how he must have fumed! All they were concerned with was the loss of a stable and barn which had burnt down, and a tenant farmer who had left without paying the rent. Rimbaud's sister Vitalie recorded his home-coming in her diary:

> That day was to mark an epoch in my life, for it saw an event of profound significance. My second brother arrived home without warning. I can still see myself in our room, where my brother, sister and mother were arranging some of our things. We heard a light knock on the door. I went to answer it . . . imagine my surprise, I found myself face to face with Arthur. When we had recovered from the first moments of astonishment, he explained to us the reason for his visit; we were delighted, and he participated in our pleasure. We spent the day together, showing Arthur the farm, which he hardly knew.

Rimbaud's return was not so much a home-coming as an enforced necessity. He returned home when he was either desperate or frightened. And he was certainly the latter. Drug addiction and the pathological symptoms of withdrawal were little understood at this time. Laudanum, which includes tincture of opium, was used as a general anodyne in the nineteenth century. Coleridge, De Quincey, Baudelaire and many others became hooked on opium after first using it as a sedative or pain-killer. Rimbaud used drugs as still another incentive to vision. Lack of bodily awareness and any literature on dependency made the taking of hard drugs seem an experiment without liability. Withdrawal clinics were to be a thing of the future. Rimbaud had to write *Une saison en enfer* as part of the process of detoxification. He had to suffer the attendant symptoms at Roche: muscular contraction, hallucination, panic, thirst, paranoia, delirium. So far as we know, he lay on his bed all day, refused to eat, suffered constant insomnia and was remote, withdrawn into his inner conflict. He probably tramped around the nearby countryside, confused by what was happening to him, unable to seek medical help and raging against the misfortune that had reduced him to such a state of intense suffering. It was at this time that he began work on *Une saison en enfer*, ostensibly with the hope of earning himself some money from a short prose book, but also with the intention of externalizing his madness, his poetic method. And by 1873 Rimbaud had authority. At eighteen he was able to look back on a devotion to poetry so intense that in its short duration it seemed to have carried a past inheritance and to extend into an illimitable future. Rimbaud's valediction to poetry establishes the premises for a post-millennial, twenty-first-century poetics.

Verlaine was at Jehonville. His life was ruined. Rimbaud was at Roche. He was burning in a crucible of pain. When he smashed the wall, he broke his hand open. Blood. He did not want to shout. His sister's shadow was outside the door, too frightened to knock. Faces seen at the London docks flashed up. Now he knew. They too were hooked. Grey faces. Contracted pupils. The shakes. DELIRIUM. Image after image. Constriction of the diaphragm. Irregular heart-beat, his breathing laboured. Nausea. Pain turning in on pain. Conscious or unconscious, the same hallucinated threat. A wolf licked his face; a jackal eviscerated him. Now they were speaking outside. His mother, the police, Verlaine. Verlaine was showing them the knife-marks on his chest. They were throwing sand over his body. Burying him in this room. Sand that would seal up his mouth, pour out of his nostrils.

Something of Rimbaud's state of mind at this time is expressed in a letter he wrote to Delahaye in May, a month after his arrival at Roche:

> What a shit hole! and what naïve monsters these peasants are. At night, if you want a drink, you have to walk miles. The *mother* has sunk me in this hellish place.
>
> I don't know how to get out of it: but I shall. I miss that atrocious Charlestown, the [Café] Universe, the library, etc. . . . I am working quite steadily though; I am writing little prose stories, general title: Pagan Book or Negro Book. It is

crazy and innocent. O innocence! innocence, innocence, innoc . . . shit!

Verlaine must have imposed on you the unenviable task of arguing with Devin, the printer of the *Nôress*. I think this Devin could do Verlaine's book reasonably and quite satisfactorily. (As long as he doesn't use the shitty type that goes into his newspaper. He's even capable of pasting an advertisement on it!)

I have nothing more to tell you, the contemplation of nature fills up my arse. I am yours, o Nature, o my mother!

Hope to see you soon. I am doing everything I can to make a reunion possible.

R.

I've reopened my letter. Verlaine seems to have proposed a rendezvous for Sunday the 18th, in Boulion. I can't go. If you do, he will probably give you some prose pieces of mine or his, for safe return.

Mother Rimb. will return to Charlestown some time in June. This is certain, and I shall try to stay in that pretty town for a while.

The sun is incandescent, no matter the freezing mornings. The day before yesterday I went to see the Prussians at Vouziers, a subprefecture of 10,000 people, seven kilom. from here. That cheered me up.

I am out of my mind. Not a book, not a bar within reach, not even a street incident. What a horror the French countryside is! My future depends on this book, for which half a dozen stories have still to be invented. How can I invent atrocities here? I can't send you any of the stories, although I already have three, *that costs too much*! That's it for now. . . .

At the time of writing this letter, Rimbaud was far from renouncing the idea of literature. Presumably he looked to the embryonic book as a source of income that would allow him to write and travel. It was not until the autumn of 1873 that he turned against the source of his inspiration. Something of the naïvety that counterbalanced his extraordinary precocity is manifested in his youthful hope that his Negro Book would sell.

Even Charleville, the provincial town that Rimbaud so loathed, seemed an oasis compared with the desolate flatlands around Roche. Rimbaud was fuming, and he wrote his best when his inner momentum reached a pitch of violence. He seems to have written 'Mauvais sang' and 'Alchimie du verbe', two of the most potent constituents of *Une saison en enfer*, during this period of withdrawal. 'Mauvais sang' is furiously confessional, its strength lying in the interleaving of fiction and autobiography. Rimbaud creates both a mythic and a real self and both are imaginative projections. It is impossible to write about the self without lying. Language creates its own fiction, it is both a centring in truth and an instrument of deflection. And above all it creates associations within the work, the metaphorical leaps that function within a field of their own autonomous making.

. . . On the roads, on winter nights, without shelter, without clothes, without bread, a voice gripped my frozen heart: 'Weakness or strength: you exist, that is strength. You don't know where you are going or why you are going, go in everywhere, answer everything. They won't kill you any more than if you were a corpse.' In the morning I had so vacant a look and such a dead face, that those I met *perhaps did not see me*.

In cities, the mud would suddenly appear red and black, like a mirror when a lamp in the next room moves, like a treasure in the forest! Good luck, I cried, and I saw a sea of flames and smoke in the sky; and, to right, to left, all wealth detonated like a billion thunderbolts. . . .

Something of Rimbaud's openness to all experience and the self-questioning voice he encountered in the conflict between I and the other is brought out here in his fearless confrontation with the unknown. He is the prophet passing through cities. His magical properties and dissipation are such that he goes invisible. And wherever he goes, there are signs: the sky breaks into flames. Over his shoulder he observes the pyrotechnic combustion of thunderbolts. He hallucinates the fiction of his becoming. His vengeance is upon capitalism, that system which denies the individual the right to live by means of creative choice and expression, and instead demands that he prostitutes himself to an institution for money. Rimbaud's rage is the measure of the suffering he has undergone in order to pursue his life as a *voyant*. A poet's survival is chance if he remains true to his calling.

> . . . Yes, my eyes are closed to your light. I am an animal, a negro. But I can be saved. You are false negroes, maniacs, savages, misers all of you. Merchant, you are a nigger; magistrate, you are a nigger; general, you are a nigger; emperor, scabby old faggot, you are a nigger: you have drunk untaxed liquor from Satan's still. – This people is inspired by fever and cancer. Invalids and old men are so respectable that they ask to be boiled. – The best thing is to leave this continent where madness prowls searching for hostages for these wretches. I will enter into the true kingdom of the sons of Ham.

Rimbaud is always moving on; not even poetry can restrain him, anchor him to any sense of territory gained. He is always in the process of leaving. The world is too small even when it is multiplied by the imagination. And this hunger for new worlds which informs his poetry expresses not only a dissatisfaction with his provincial upbringing but an objection to the limitations imposed by the universe. And *Une saison en enfer* reflects Rimbaud's impatience with almost every line won. He is bored by the image he has minted. His reaction is immediately to attack it. He is forever severing the link by which the snake's head intersects with its tail.

In the six weeks that Rimbaud was at Roche, with Verlaine across the border, he was creating by way of the method he was in the process of renouncing. In 'Mauvais sang' he writes: 'Boredom no longer attracts me. Rage, debauchery, madness, of which I know all the elations and disasters, – my whole burden is laid aside. Without losing our minds, let us evaluate the extent of my innocence. I should no longer find comfort in asking to be whipped. I have embarked on a wedding with Jesus Christ as father-in-law.'

Rimbaud writes with the authority of one who has suffered and entered into all possible states of derangement. And there is such huge isolation in his undertaking. His contemporaries were busy writing verse, that rational undertaking which operates within the approved boundaries of social consciousness. Rimbaud sat in the centre of the circle in flames. As a schoolboy he had seen through the limitations of that conventional effete – the man who retires to the comfort of his study and therapeutically devotes an occasional hour of emotional disquiet to the composition of poetry. He could ridicule these men because they had risked nothing, and, even if his life entailed rejection and anonymity, he had lived. He had walked through the furnace shrieking: 'I am alive in ways that you will never know.'

In 'Alchimie du verbe' Rimbaud relates 'L'histoire d'une de mes folies'. The poem is an exegesis of his self-induced supraconscious faculties. Rimbaud tells us, in so far as he can ever eliminate deception, of his poetic discoveries. Written in the past tense, it is the most extraordinary summation of a revolutionary poetics.

> . . . I invented the colour of the vowels! – *A* black, *E* white, *I* red, *O* blue, *U* green. – I regulated the form and movement of each consonant, and, with instinctive rhythms, I boasted of inventing a poetic language accessible, one day or another, to all the senses. I reserved translation rights.
>
> At first this was a study. I wrote of silences and of nights, I recorded the inexpressible. I described vertiginous states of madness. . . .

Rimbaud is referring here to his poem 'Voyelles', but more than that he is making an unmitigated claim to have invented a new language.

Critics have argued variously that 'Voyelles' owes its inception to an alphabet with coloured letters used amongst French children during the Second Empire, to the permutations of alchemical colours from black to white to yellow to red, or (Pierre Petitfils's theory) that the sonnet is indebted to musical chromaticism, and the piano lessons that Rimbaud received from Ernest Cabaner at the Hôtel des Etrangers during his Paris stay in 1871. Of these theories the latter seems most probable, and more likely to have corresponded to Rimbaud's search for a universal language. By the time Huysmans came to write *À rebours*, synaesthesia, whereby sense associations find a corresponding and collective synthesis, was considered to be the apogee of symbolist experiment. Whatever the germinative seed of Rimbaud's sonnet, it is the accidental connections as a result of inspiration which succeed in conveying to the poem its oddness and originality. And in 'Alchimie du verbe' Rimbaud vindicates his method as one of omniscient inspiration. He is the creator of his poetic universe; the ancillary things that have prompted poems are filtered out as the imagination takes over. *Une saison en enfer* pivots on I – the poetico-centric universe. Rimbaud is both talking to himself and others. And the intensity of what he reveals to himself demands that we listen. His poetry is like the beat of a drum that sounds on the earth's crust.

... I accustomed myself to pure hallucination: I saw very clearly a mosque in place of a factory, a drummers' school made up of angels, carriages on roads in the sky, a drawing-room at the bottom of a lake; monsters, mysteries; a vaudeville's title evoked terror in me.

Then I explained my magic sophisms by the hallucination of words!

I ended up by looking on my mental disorder as sacred. I was idle, a prey to heavy fever: I envied the happiness of animals – caterpillars, which represent the innocence of limbo, and moles, the sleep of virginity! ...

It is no less awesome now, than at the moment of creation, that an eighteen-year-old suffering from drug withdrawal and isolated in a barn at Roche should have found a tone so authoritative in its evaluation, appraisal and dismissal of a poetic method as to carry a conviction so unfaltering that the work reads with the gravity of the great poetic scriptures, the Upanishads, the Gita and the parables of the New Testament. The voice is already unrepeatable: it is so great that it arrests further achievement. Rimbaud is the magus who exalts in extinguishing his own power. It is a fire-dance, each step one of immense provocation because he will never go back to the place he has left. And he is the sole witness of the psychodrama acted out in *Une saison en enfer*. While he is writing the poem, and even in the act of making a valediction to poetry, he is still the creator. We experience him daring the edge. He does not yet know what it is like to live without creativity, to step out of the circle into chaos. And it was not until the autumn that he was to renounce poetry. What Rimbaud underwent in April and May was the agonized elation of knowing he had taken a method to its last frontier. The step beyond that may have led to pathological insanity; a psychosis precluding voluntary return. The barn in which Rimbaud locked himself away, shutting out the light that would be painful to his contracted pupils, was both a metaphorical threshing-floor and the contained cell within which the mystic or madman experiences vision. Rimbaud had taken on the responsibility of a shaman within a society that offered no support for the role. And this continues to be the discomforting social reprisal that the committed poet faces. A material world has rejected vision, prophetic speech and oneiric enlightenment so totally that the artist finds no help either psychologically or financially for the risk incurred by his undertaking. The imagination has come increasingly to find its support in the world of psychoanalysis and psychopathology, schools of thought that in dealing with disturbance and obsessive inner states have found themselves inextricably linked with the stuff of creative expression.

Of his delirium, Rimbaud writes in 'Alchimie du verbe':

... None of the sophistries of madness – the madness that gets locked up – was forgotten by me: I could say to them all again, I have the system.

My health was threatened. Terror came upon me. I would fall into heavy sleeps which lasted several days, and, when I woke up, my bad dreams continued. I was ripe for death, and my weakness led me down dangerous roads to the edge of the world and Cimmeria, a land of darkness and whirlwinds. ...

I find Rimbaud's hell or encounter with madness more convincing than Dante's *Inferno* with its emphasis on physical retribution as a source of continuous suffering in death. Rimbaud's infernal states are spontaneously evoked; they are part of the modern psyche with its incorporation of drug experience and chaotic personal fragmentation, and most importantly the alienation of the creative individual in the face of material capitalism. Rimbaud is so much a part of the catastrophic momentum of the twentieth century that his poetry marches hand in hand with the future. And in many ways we are all confronted with a spiritual desert, an exodus towards the waste places which reflect our depleted inner reserves.

In 'Alchimie du verbe' Rimbaud confronts the notion of multiple lives. We are one and many. Our ability to create alternative lives for ourselves is constant. We invent the fiction we adopt each day. I am one and many. We are all in states of metamorphosis, either conscious or unconscious. Most of us realize the alternative selves we might have had. The options are numerous; we have somehow to elect a choice which seems most fully to realize the potential within us. And we have empathy, which is a transferable quality. We can think ourselves into what it is like to be an animal, another person, the opposite sex, and if the need to identify with another life becomes obsessive, we can act out the part. Rimbaud evokes this state of confusion and in doing so has us question the premises of self-identity.

... To each being it seemed to me that several *other* lives were due. This man does not know what he is doing: he is an angel. This family is a pack of dogs. In front of several men, I talked out loud with a moment out of one of their other lives. – In that way, I have loved a pig. ...

In states of acute nervous crisis I have seen similar metamorphoses take place. There was a man I knew whose unresolved and tormented homosexuality manifested itself for me in the manner of seeing him as a failed woman. One breast was tucked into a low-cut white satin dress. Anxious as he was to divest himself of this uncomfortable role, his image changed to that of a wolf challenging the night from a rocky place in the hills. And who was I in his eyes? And so on. Madness comes about when we accept a misidentity for a permanence.

By this time both Rimbaud and Verlaine were bored by inaction. Verlaine seems to have accepted that the fissure which had opened between him and his wife was now unbridgeable, and Rimbaud was seeking any distraction which would free him from the monotony of the countryside around Roche. These two figures, who by rights should not have met again, were now hurried back into a false union which was to explode into an almost homicidal mania by midsummer.

By way of Liège and Antwerp, the two travellers set sail for Harwich and, after making their way back to London, rented a room at 8 Great College Street in Camden Town. Still living on the generosity of Madame Verlaine, they once again entertained the idea of giving French lessons to private pupils. These were crazy times. They overreached circumspection and had it known to the Communards in London that theirs was a sexual relationship. Rumour was abroad of 'unspeakable relations'.

Rimbaud smashed the mirror with his fist. Verlaine had ruined his life. He could never embark on a literary career. He took a glass splinter and jabbed it into his wrist. Nothing happened. Verlaine, rising from a drunken sleep, went for him, hands reaching for his throat, only to be repulsed by a violent kick in the groin.

Rimbaud cursed everything that had made his life into a condition of torment: his mother, his father, his upbringing, his alcoholic lover, the brutal solitude that came from living in London, the insults he had received when first he went to Paris, the disparagement meted out to his poetry, the black wall that opposed his future. Verlaine would have throttled both Rimbaud and Mathilde with his right and left hands. Each of them had contributed to his ruin, his volatile alcoholism. He wanted his mother's comfort, a new beginning in which he was free to choose a way of life suited to his indecisive and overwrought sensibility. If he stepped back far enough, the shadows in his life might disappear. Rimbaud hated everyone. They had all tricked him. He had expected so much; and he had ended up poor, reviled, inescapably a product of his peasant upbringing. He struck his boot against a wall, wishing it was Verlaine's face.

Verlaine could not see a way out. Rimbaud, Mathilde, his mother: something had to happen. If only he were rich, had fame or a means of escape. He was writing again, but the relationship had been deleterious to his creativity. Rimbaud was too powerful. He had lost the confidence to write. He had tried for a self-obliterative sensuality; and now that too had disappeared. It was blood on the walls, knife-marks tattooing the chest and ribs.

At the time, Rimbaud's mind must have been explosive with *Une saison en enfer*. But London was not the place to engage in a poem that owed its origins to a ferocious confrontation with his childhood, occult beliefs, ancestors, homosexuality and drug addiction. He needed to root this poem in the securely indigenous. As is so often the way, the return to an inherited physical landscape provided the poet with the tension necessary to promote extreme psychic risk. The tumbledown barn at Roche was to become the stage for Rimbaud's universal drama. He needed constriction against which to rage.

Both men were near to desperation. Rimbaud, for all his arrogant defiance and seeming indifference to suffering, hated cities. He preferred to be out on the road, embracing the future under the empty spaces of the skyline. The oppressive streets of Camden Town, the invincible xenophobia manifested by the English, the lack of café life, all of these things must have been additionally hard for him to bear. I imagine Rimbaud as frightened and vulnerable. He must have been excitably paranoid, for he was after all engaging in illicit sex and taking drugs, which could have led to his arrest. And there was the constant lack of money as well as the internal doubts as to the efficacy of his poetic method. What did life want of him? Why was he different? He had gone along with the inner voice and it had ruined him. And there was something about the nature of his experience that presented insurmountable obstacles to the future. What was it? Had he lived all his life already? The shadow was big. It had dropped on him in April at Roche, but he had warded off its pernicious presence by celebrating his destruction in poetry. Yet now it had returned. A rift in him was opening. He must have feared for his sanity. Opium was beginning to generate involuntary visions in him. He had almost kicked the habit in the painful withdrawal months of April and May; and now he could not tell whether he had started smoking again or if the flash-backs were as a consequence of narcotic poisoning. There was another world going on somewhere else. Had he not written 'La vraie vie est absente'? What he saw now were nations in the sky, a black ape frozen into coitus with a white girl in a solid block of ice, flames raging in the streets, crewless ships drifting into fog, Verlaine's open mouth revolving like a whirlpool, sucking the room in, swallowing the bed, the wardrobe, and Rimbaud was suddenly a little green frog hopping to meet the quickening revolutions of that insanely stretched mouth. And when he dived in he was swallowed by a cavernous hall. His mother was sitting naked on a block of stone. She was writing down his thoughts. She knew them without his having to speak. She knew everything: their sex habits, their theft, their mad ravings, their knife fights. When she looked up at her son, her mouth became a snake's head and tail at the corners. And there were people watching up in the gallery. They stood with their heads bowed, their wrists in manacles. Drops of blood fell from a great height. He had to avoid them, for they burnt a hole into the floor and hissed fiercely on contact with stone. Their blood was molten; and all the time his mother went on taking down his thoughts. And now she was writing with blood. It was his own. She dipped her nib into a wrist vein. He felt nothing. She was going to use him up, carry on writing until his eight pints of blood were spread in parallel lines across reams of paper. It went on drop by red drop. . . .

Something had to break. Verlaine still imagined he would find sympathy in Mathilde; he continued to delude himself that he had only to renounce Rimbaud and the immediate reparation of his marriage would ensue. He saw his wife as malleable, pusillanimous, pliant to his needs, but it was a delusion fostered by absinthe and a tedious egomania.

'If only you knew how fucking silly you look with that herring in your hand.' Rimbaud shouted this out of the window as Verlaine was returning home with a herring in one hand and a bottle of salad oil in the other. It was fuel for conflagration.

Unknown to Rimbaud, Verlaine had been planning his departure for weeks. He was looking for the smallest legitimate provocation to erupt. His case was packed and ready. Something of Rimbaud's drug estrangement is evident in the way that he had failed to notice Verlaine's plans for an imminent departure. They were clearly living in very different mental spaces. But Verlaine was gone. Travelling either by bus or underground he got to St Catherine's Wharf for the Antwerp boat. There was a delay before the full force of the shock hit Rimbaud and, travelling in pursuit, unable to believe that Verlaine had acted so finally on what was after all no more than a customary altercation, he arrived to see the boat weighing anchor. Verlaine was probably drunk. He could make no decision without anaesthetizing himself with alcohol. His plan was to call a meeting with his wife in Brussels. If that failed, he would blow his brains out. Whether this action was intended for Mathilde or Rimbaud is unclear. And because Verlaine suffered from DT, no one was prepared to believe it.

Rimbaud found himself deserted in London. He was left without money or provisions, thrown in again upon himself and faced with the inexhaustible need to find material support for his life of spiritual aspiration. Often it is hard to find the money even for a bus-fare. The editorial whiz-kid sprinting up from the provinces to London in a BMW, would be unaware that Rimbaud's destitute predicament can inflict anyone who pursues poetry as a commitment and not an avocation.

Broken down, threatened by everything inside and out, Rimbaud wrote a letter (4 July 1873) intended for Verlaine:

Come back, come back, dear friend, my only friend, come back. I swear I'll be kind. If I was mad with you, it was only a joke, and one I couldn't stop. I am more sorry than words can ever say. Come back, everything will be forgotten. How terrible that you should have taken that joke seriously. For two days I haven't stopped crying. Come back. Be brave, dear friend. Nothing is lost. You have only to make another journey. We'll live here again, courageously and patiently. Ah! I beg you. It's for your good, too. Come back, you'll find all your things here.

I hope you realize now that there was nothing serious in our argument. What a terrible moment! But why didn't you come when I signalled to you to get off the boat? Have we lived together for two years to come to this! What are you going to do? If you don't want to come back here, would you like me to come to you?

Yes, I was in the wrong.

Oh! you won't forget me will you?

No, you can't forget me.

As for me, I still have you here.

Listen, answer your friend, aren't we to carry on living together?

Be brave. Reply to me quickly.

I can't stay here much longer.

Don't read this except whole-heartedly.

Quick, tell me if I must come to you.

Yours, all my life.

Rimbaud must have feared madness. There is a love that comes from incompatibility, both partners fearing to exchange the irreconcilable for the unknown. Everything in their lives together must have streamed through Rimbaud's consciousness with extraordinary clarity. The tempestuous audacity of their initial love, things said and done, hopes, aspirations, poverty, humour, despair, viciousness, brutality, accusations, and always the face of Mathilde, Verlaine's wife who had so often interposed in their relationship. Verlaine hated her but he blamed Rimbaud for implanting that emotion in him. And was he not made to feel a failure because he lacked characteristics that Verlaine had known in his wife? They could never be happy because Verlaine had known and loved this woman.

For the first few hours Verlaine's absence was an unreality. There had to be a mistake. He would be back on the next crossing. But Rimbaud had insufficient money to wait. Whatever their differences there had always been two of them; one could protect the other. Now there was nothing but this huge fear enveloping him, picking him up in its talons, threatening to suffocate him. Rimbaud was paralysed. The only place that offered respite was home, but how could he get there? He was convulsing. What if he lost his mind and found himself homeless and without identity in the underground? Even the prospect of Roche and his unwelcoming mother must have been consolatory. And when one is hysterical, which means in inner flight, one imagines that one can get to a place just by thinking oneself there. Rimbaud must have thought of the leaky old barn where his presence scared rats, of the old days in Charleville when he and Delahaye were free to roam the countryside and imagine a future that was still open-ended. But his had happened. He had run clean up against a wall. He was trapped in a sticky black net. It was tightening over him so that he could not breathe. And the terrible poverty of the room and house. He was going crazy and Verlaine wasn't there to listen or to receive the blame.

He wanted to scream and he did. There was a knock at the door. For a moment he thought it was Verlaine. He was back again. And since the marvellous occurred in his poetry all the time, he had no need to ask questions. Instead it was a threatening English voice, telling him that if he didn't quieten down, the police would be called. The police? They would want to know the nature of his relationship with Verlaine, they would search for drugs.

The evening and the night must have been relentless, implacable, interminable. There was nothing he could do but sit like a red-eyed beast in his lair and wait for the morning. And the next day Verlaine's letter arrived, full of the sentimentality which was inseparable from his nature. He threatened suicide. 'If three days from now I'm not reconciled with my wife, in perfect conditions, I'm going to blow my brains out. . . . My last thought will be for you, for you who were calling me, this afternoon, from the quayside, when I wouldn't return, because it is necessary that I should die.'

Rimbaud found himself once again the victim of Verlaine's deluded belief that he could resume his former married life simply by appearing to renounce his homosexuality. But Mathilde had no intention of hurrying to reunite with a man who had once set fire to her hair, beaten her up physically and dashed their child against a wall. Verlaine had been given chances and on each occasion he had burnt his boats. Mathilde would leave him to the reflection of flames on a black night sea.

Verlaine's mother rushed to Brussels to be with her son. And Rimbaud's mother, informed of the situation by Verlaine, wrote to him (6 July 1873) with an emotional honesty and inspiritment that suggests levels of compassion she was never to show her son.

> Kill yourself, unfortunate man! To kill oneself at a time of extreme crisis is an act of *cowardice*; but to commit suicide when one has a loving mother, who would give her life for you, who will die of your death, and when one is also the father of a young boy . . . to kill oneself in these circumstances is infamy. . . .
>
> Monsieur, I do not know the nature of your quarrel with Arthur; but I always knew that your relationship would end disastrously. Why? you will ask me. Because what is not authorized by good and honest parents cannot possibly bring happiness to the children.

How much did she know? From the nature of her letter, it seems everything. It is much to her credit that she delivers no moral imprecations against homosexuality. Possibly her experience of life with her husband had clouded her views of heterosexual relations, and in a perverse way she warmed to her son's attraction to his own sex. If Rimbaud's relationship had been with a girl, and therefore a rival to Madame Rimbaud's psychological regime, doubtless she would have maintained an impenetrable silence. She would have disowned her son and considered her parental duties ended. But with a man it was different. She had corresponded with Verlaine in London and seemed prepared to overlook his alcoholism and ambivalent sexuality. And her feeling towards both him and her son is that they are children. The disciplinarian in her advised Verlaine to pull himself together: 'You must also apply yourself to work, find a purpose in life; you will naturally have many bad days still to go through; but however disillusioned you may be with men, never despair of God. Believe me, he alone knows how to comfort and heal.'

One wishes only that she could have found it in her heart to write her son a similar letter.

But Verlaine was sobering up. Suicide is an irrevocable act; it was not in his nature to make incisive decisions. He could imagine himself dead and conceive of the subsequent guilt incurred by both Mathilde and Rimbaud. Yet he would not be there to experience it. He would like to have had them believe he was dead, only to reappear and find himself the subject of profound sympathy. But of course the latter was not possible. Still intent on acting out a drama, on 8 July he wired Rimbaud to come to Brussels, Hôtel Liégeois, as he Verlaine was about to go to Spain to enlist as a volunteer in the Carlist ranks. This scheme was a way of maintaining dramatic action – Verlaine was on the edge of the heroic or cataclysmic, as he saw it – and Rimbaud must be made to suffer for having pushed him to such extremes.

And the plot succeeded. On the proceeds of selling their clothes and a few possessions, Rimbaud arrived in Brussels on 9 July, Verlaine having meanwhile moved into the Hôtel de la Ville de Courtrai in the centre of the city. Rimbaud found himself once again faced by Verlaine and a woman, only this time it was the latter's mother and not his wife. He sensed that he was to be the subject of humiliation and all of his prickly, obstinate Cuif blood rose to the defensive. To counteract Verlaine's drunken scheme of enlisting, he had decided that his future lay in returning to Paris. To have said Charleville would have been to admit defeat. And, anyhow, he had not given Paris a sufficient try. During his stay there in 1872 he had been angry, destitute, engaged in a process of sensory derangement. He had wanted to outrage the literary world and he had succeeded in his design. Perhaps he hoped that the book he had begun in April and May would establish his name as a poet. He would show Verlaine that he could succeed alone. His genius was meteoric; it would light up the century.

But for the moment Rimbaud was trapped. The presence of Verlaine's mother prevented honesty of expression. And there was a rift. Perhaps for a time he felt strong in the belief that he would regain his independence and be free of Verlaine's lachrymose dypsomania. But Verlaine was not going to make things easy. He wanted to force the issue; he was drunk, belligerent and looking to blame Rimbaud for the dissolution of his marriage and his premature redundancy as a poet. The night was taken up in bitter argument, in as much as Rimbaud could attempt to reason with a man who was little more than a gelatinous sponge of absinthe. Something of the twisted fury of their love is evident in the emotional deadlock. Neither wanted to be the first to break, although this time Rimbaud must have been firm in his intention to leave for Paris the next day. He must have been nervous, urinating excessively, breaking out into cold sweats from the absence of drugs, strung out over the void on a breaking thread. When Verlaine passed out from alcohol there was the long summer night to endure, broken by snatches of sleep, livid hallucinations, panic that the next day would be a repetition of what they had already suffered.

The next day Verlaine went out early. He had noticed a gunsmith's shop in the Passage des Galeries St Hubert. We know from the evidence given at the trial that he purchased a 7 mm, six-cylinder revolver and a box of fifty cartridges. He spent the morning drinking and loaded the revolver in the latrine of the Café Rue des Chartreux. We do not know whom he intended to shoot; but it was an accelerative step to the momentum of his Brussels drama. Whatever he did, news of it would get back to Mathilde. It might finally persuade her to come to his assistance.

Rimbaud was resolute. He would leave for Paris at ten to four. He wanted to be out of it. Verlaine was still whipping himself into an intoxicated fury, locking Rimbaud in the hotel room and going out for another drink to fortify his courage. Verlaine's mother interceded once and offered to pay Rimbaud's train-fare to Paris. Time was running out. Three-thirty. There was less than twenty minutes dividing Verlaine from a blank, loveless future. He had to make an example of someone for the losses he had suffered. In his fury, he blamed this obstinate peasant boy, so intractable in his obduracy, for inciting him to this savage retribution.

There was fierce shouting. Neither would concede. Verlaine locked the door. 'Now try to go!' he threatened Rimbaud. And something in him snapped. A red tiger raced through his blood. He fired three shots. The first hit Rimbaud in the left wrist, while the other two went wide and embedded themselves in the wall.

Verlaine promptly ran into his mother's room and threw himself on her bed. It must have been huge in his head. Homicide. Mania. Rimbaud's face breaking up like a red meringue. But it was only his wrist, although the bleeding was copious. When Rimbaud appeared, Verlaine threw the gun at his feet saying: 'Here, unload it in my temple.'

Rimbaud was taken off to St John's Hospital where his wound was treated and bandaged. No one in the hotel seemed to have heard anything, and Rimbaud's injury was explained away as an accident. The gun had automated itself while Verlaine was cleaning it. No one at the hospital could have believed this. The sort of violent altercation that had occurred lives as a charge, a current on the skin. It is there as an animation in the voice, a dilation of the pupils. Verlaine's mother must have told the lie with her anxiety over her son's unpredictable conduct. There is reason to believe that both Verlaine and Rimbaud had become seriously disturbed in the course of their relationship. Their injurious knife fights, their respective states of intoxication – Verlaine blind drunk on absinthe and Rimbaud spaced out on drugs, or drugs and liquor combined – had created a legacy of estrangement and mutual friction. Now the storm was about to break. Verlaine still wanted something. If it wasn't homicide, then it had to be an act of demonstrative violence. Was he trying to prove to his mother that he was a reluctant homosexual? A gun is also by metaphorical extension a phallus. There is nothing more counterproductive to sexual performance than constant inebriation. Verlaine had an infallible substitute, a weapon that would not become flaccid, and one that could kill. And no one thought to disarm him.

Rimbaud meanwhile had decided he would return to Roche and not Paris. He had just suffered the deep trauma of being shot. He wanted to go home, to be amongst familiar things, to be with his mother. Verlaine's mother gave him the twenty francs for the journey. She must already have feared legal recriminations. Madame Rimbaud was not likely to accept the calculated mendacity that her son had been shot accidentally. Why did Verlaine have a gun, anyhow? Wouldn't any mother ask that question? Things were fraught, tetchy; the air crackled with tension. Rimbaud was in a state of paranoid fear. This madman might level the gun at his eyes and blast him through his head. Whatever was fuelling Verlaine was still injecting red-hot adrenalin into his system. They began their walk to the station. Verlaine would be left with nothing. He knew Rimbaud would never come back, that this time things had gone too far. It would be better if they were both dead, but the same old problem arose. Verlaine needed the satisfaction of knowing what he had done. He couldn't count on that in death. The volitional control he had over his life would be extinguished. They continued towards the Gare du Midi. By ten to eight they had reached the Place Rouppe. Verlaine was running out of time. The clock hands were suddenly attached to his heart. They would remain fixed there. He took the gun out of his pocket, vehemently, maniacally, and shouted to Rimbaud that he was going to blow his brains out. Rimbaud jumped to one side and took off in the direction of the nearest policeman and implored help. 'He wants to kill me,' he shouted, pointing at Verlaine.

Verlaine was arrested and taken to the central police station at the Hôtel de Ville. Rimbaud, who was in a state of fever as a result of the bullet still lodged in his wrist, was admitted into hospital the following day and stayed there a week suffering from exhaustion.

DELIRIUM. The imploded had built to an external explosion. The hysterical nature of their relationship had been revealed to the world through a bullet. What was private, dangerously precarious in its lethal potential, had through an impassioned action entered the public domain. Verlaine was being held on a charge of attempted murder, a sentence which would later be commuted owing to Rimbaud's evidence in court and his desire to drop all criminal charges. But the scandal had broken. Rimbaud was only eighteen. He had lived so fast, so intensely, and now he had to face an interrogation by authorities convinced from the start of his homosexual relations with Verlaine.

Unable to leave his bed, because of the high fever from which he was suffering, Rimbaud was visited by the examining magistrate. What we know of the emotional turbulence of his brief encounter with Verlaine in Brussels comes from the evidence given in his statement.

Q: On what did you live in London?

R: Largely on the money that Madame Verlaine sent to her son. We also gave French lessons together, but these brought in practically nothing. Perhaps twelve francs a week, towards the end.

Q: Are you aware of the reasons for the dissension between the accused and his wife?

R: Verlaine didn't want his wife to continue living with her parents.

Q: Did she not list your intimacy with Verlaine as the cause for separation?

R: Yes, she accuses us of immoral relations, but I shall not even bother to contradict such calumny.

The bullet was extracted on 17 July. On 19 July Rimbaud, fearing the severe sentence that would be imposed on Verlaine, made an act of renunciation. He declared that he was convinced that when Verlaine purchased the weapon he had no criminal intentions, and that the latter's action was the result of intoxication. But the revocation was unsatisfactory and came too late. Verlaine was brought before the court on 28 July and again on 8 August. He was sentenced to two years' imprisonment and ordered to pay a fine of two hundred francs. Rimbaud stayed on in Brussels to hear the verdict and then made his way back on foot to Roche. He was shattered. Lack of nutrition and proper care meant that his wrist was still painful. Paterne Berrichon tells us that he was led by police to the border and tramped back to Roche.

Everything must have been blown up to huge proportions in his mind: Verlaine's face, the sound of the gunshots reverberating in his head, the blood streaming from his wrist on to the floor. To get back and write about it was the only way he could elucidate his journey through the visionary hells. He had survived the physical experience, now he had to resume battle with the hallucinated fire he had lit in April. It was raging; and his book would be called *Une saison en enfer*.

Chapter Five

Torrid dog-days. The air siccative, the Ardennes unrelieved – a sky in which each oblong white cloud appeared as a messenger from the real world. Rimbaud's hand was bandaged, his arm in a sling. The hole in his wrist, like that in the young soldier's side in 'Le Dormeur du val', was a fierce reminder of the shaman's mortality. It was a symbolic wound. The external could encroach on the internal; the incursion had marked him. A wound is a tear in the cosmic seam. Rimbaud was split open to the world. He had once again to retaliate by way of a defensive, and *Une saison en enfer* was his weapon.

Rimbaud's papers had been confiscated by the Belgian police. We do not know how much of the origins of *Une saison en enfer* was lost; we shall never know Rimbaud's entire poetic output. He did not care to collect it, and his life was itinerant. We have to imagine it, and the books he may have written are the ones we are still hoping to write. Ultimate vision, ultimate audacity, ultimate temerity. The poet as one who takes on the unknown. Octavio Paz says: 'Poetry either leaps into the unknown or it is nothing.'

Shock induces a state of dissociation, disorientation. Rimbaud was out of it on his return to Roche. His past had exploded into flames, his present was intolerable and the anticipation of the future demanded that he change his life. What he suffered from was exposure. You cannot disguise a wound or the questions it provokes. Nor can you escape from a small family on a farm in Roche. There were eyes everywhere at the table. His mother's,

94

and those of his sisters Vitalie and Isabelle, and those belonging to his brother Frédéric. They were busy with the harvest. It was live or die – the vocabulary of the land. There was hay to be brought in, there were corn sheaves to be gathered. But his wound kept him apart. It argued for the sanctuary he needed in order to write. In the journal that Vitalie kept, she noted: 'My brother Arthur did not participate in the farmwork; he found sufficient occupation with his pen to prevent him sharing in our manual labours.'

Rimbaud needed to be alone. Was he not engaged in writing a poem that oscillated between the immediacy of experience and the refutation of the confessional mode in which he had cast his poem? He had discovered a method of detonating the line. His images flashed with a high nervous charge. It was like being shot again each time he found the right image.

It was dark inside the barn. He could smell the sweat on his unwashed clothes. The sunlight chinked as tangible gold threads on the straw. His metabolism was in revolt. There were neither drugs nor alcohol to hand at the farm. Words were the only means of stabilizing his craziness. That or shouting out his pain. And he had known so much: his life had been exceptional for an eighteen-year-old. And at the time of writing he must have thought that his experience would prove of vital concern to readers, even if they were shocked by his revelations. Anyhow, there was nothing else to do but write: no distractions, no friends, a blankly inhospitable landscape.

And this time his poetic rage was tempered by compassion. Had he not after all put his friend and lover in prison, after their volatile hysteria had got out of hand, and had he not ruined his life? His relationship with Verlaine was a talking-point in Paris and had now reached an epic of scandal. And yet he had not wanted all this. It must have wrung tears from his eyes as the heat furnaced in the barn. Some things just happen. You do not want them to and when you find yourself involved it is more like being a spectator to the action. You are still the same person when you walk away from an irrevocable blaze of temper. This one had involved a gun and his metacarpus. It had become public because Verlaine could not extinguish the incitement to violence. Either the gun had had to explode or his head would have. The shooting must have brought some relief, but not sufficient to curtail his homicidal impulse. If Verlaine had shot again, it would have been to kill. Rimbaud knew that. His hands shook while he wrote. The book he was writing would add some justification to his existence. He had transported it around in his head in London and Brussels, and now it would find completion in an isolation so magnified he might have been the last of his species left on earth. He could throw his visions against the cracked walls. Was he not after all confined like a madman to a cell?

Rimbaud's alchemical journey through hell, entering by the unconscious or nigredo and living within the fermenting fragmentation of his psyche, is couched in terms of the irreconcilable conflict between good and evil. Light and dark. Rimbaud's individuation rejects the circumscribed imposition of monotheism. His torment demanded search, an ongoing journey involving the excavation of inner space. He was terrified; but he had still to affirm the poet's vision as the ultimate realization of imaginative truth. And at mealtimes he remained silent. What could he say to anyone about his discoveries? His mind was still full of Verlaine, who was now undergoing the deprivation of prison life. He, Rimbaud, had been driven into hiding like an animal. Humiliated by the court and the police, he had to lie low. He was marked for what they considered to be a sexual aberration. Might they not come for him at any time, raise up the farm at night and march him off handcuffed? There was a price to pay for originality. Society seeks retribution from those who differ.

Full of contradictions and antinomies, *Une saison en enfer* is a sounding-board for all those caught up by the tide of modernity, the questioning, the scattered, the lost and above all those whose human urgency searches for a psychological meaning to life. Rimbaud attempts to break the closed circuit of life and death; he is concerned with attaining the impossible. He is both willing and reluctant to let go his hold on life and poetry. In 'L'Éclair' he writes:

What can I do? I know what work entails; and science moves too slowly. I see clearly that prayer gallops and light thunders . . . I see it clearly. It is too simple, and too unbearably hot; they will do without me. I have my duty, and I shall be proud of it in the way of several others, by putting it aside.

My life is worn out. Come! let's pretend, let's be idle, o pity! And we shall exist by amusing ourselves, by dreaming of monstrous loves and fantastic universes, complaining and quarrelling with the world's appearances, clown, vagrant, artist, bandit – priest! On my hospital bed, the smell of incense came back to me so strong; keeper of the sacred aromatics, confessor, martyr. . . .

In that I recognize my filthy upbringing. But what of it! . . . I'll let go my twenty years, if the others do likewise. . . .

No! no! at present I revolt against death. Work seems too slight to my pride: my betrayal to the world would be too brief a torment. At the last moment I would attack right and left. . . .

The contradictions are never resolved, and the poem represents the experience of living out the conflict between belief and disbelief in the validity of poetic expression. Rimbaud's poem has no subject in the sense of preconceiving a condition about which he will write. Its involvement is with immediacy and not detachment. The poem progresses according to the dictates of his psyche. It is a poem about an inner wound, and that wound is the realization that the poet has no place on earth. Capitalist ethics and nations concerned with the belligerent dominance of empires have no room for prophetic speech, oneiric journeys, the celebration of shamanism. Rimbaud's poem discovers the unrestrainable terror that has become translated into massive wars and racial persecution in the twentieth century.

It took an eighteen-year-old to do this, in a region so backward they might have stoned him for his discoveries. Rimbaud, and before him Lautréamont, was preparing the way for Freud and Jung. Together they detonated what has come to be the fall-out of the unconscious. Their powerful images remained constellated in inner space, awaiting the more clinical vocabulary that psychology was to give to the inner narrative.

Just another day. Heat. Boredom. Unaccountable mania. And although his wound had healed, a sort of shadow blood remained prominent in Rimbaud's mind. The orgasmic heat of his love for Verlaine had turned into an unalchemized, scalding reminder of his mortality – the red streamers chasing down his wrist and forming dark stars on the hotel floor. 'Hard night! The dried blood smokes on my face, and I have nothing behind me but that twisted tree! . . . Spiritual combat is as brutal as the battle of men; but the vision of justice is God's pleasure alone.'

Rimbaud's greatness lies in the fact that he went unprotected. He had nothing between him and madness but a sheet of paper. And who would understand? He knew that he was writing for future generations, sacrificing his ego for its dispersal into the collective unconscious. His work would arrive one day, but who would he be then and where would he be? Not here but over there in the ambiguity of whatever death means. *Une saison en enfer* is not only a farewell to poetry but a valediction to life.

Rimbaud never made concessions; the idealism of his youth – and he had believed absolutely in the redemptive faculty of poetry – had met with formidable opposition. At an age of expansive trust he had met with betrayal. It had started with his mother, at school even Izambard had expressed incomprehension, the poetic consensus in Paris had rejected him, and now the law had interposed between him and Verlaine.

And how has it changed? Poets may have scuttled into adopting the role of respectable bureaucrats or academics, thereby diluting their art, but the committed poet has ranged wide of these capitulations to the State and still faces the same vulnerability, the same risk, the same angular profile presented to a society seeking the round-shouldered figure of conformity.

Rimbaud's *Une saison en enfer* generates black gold. He is suspicious of the substance he has delivered. Alchemical birth involves psychophysical convulsions: delirium. The inner heat and the outer. The athanor and the golden lions of the sun. Rimbaud's pains were burns, scald-marks on his cells.

And in 'Nuit de l'enfer' Rimbaud pronounces the physical torture involved in his mystic discoveries. He has to transmute the poison within him to potable gold.

I have swallowed a terrific mouthful of poison. – Three times blessed be the idea that came to me! – My entrails are burning. The poison's violence racks my limbs, deforms me, throws me to the ground. I am dying of thirst, I am choking, I cannot cry out. This is hell, the eternal torment! Look how the fire rises! I am burning as I should. Come on, demon!

Rimbaud's encounter is that of a dervish or epileptic; one who is transported by violent physical contortion to extreme states of altered consciousness. And Rimbaud is describing a condition known and suffered. There is never exaggeration in his writing, only the realization of truth. And the getting there is always by way of the volatile present. The past is valuable to him only in so much as it intensifies the immediate. Otherwise it is dead. His is a new poetics, one that ruthlessly comments on mental and physical pain as a subject-matter which finds corroboration in the external world.

But he was writing with the awareness that he might never return to poetry. What was there to take him back? In three adolescent years he had achieved what no other poet had managed to do before him, and that is to make a poetry out of experience which might have been considered deranged or a subject for psychopathology. Neither Tasso, Hölderlin, Nerval, Baudelaire nor any of the English Romantics had dared translate madness into poetry. If they wrote about breakdown, or mental estrangement as in the case of Clare and Smart, it was with the detachment of perceiving an imbalance objectively. Rimbaud differs in that he creates a poetry out of a deranged state of mind without any such qualification. He is the least compromising poet in the history of poetry.

The hallucinations are innumerable. In truth it has always been the matter with me: no faith in history, a blank drawn over principles. I shall not enumerate on this: poets and visionaries would be jealous. I am a thousand times the richer, let me be as avaricious as the sea.

. . . I shall now unveil all mysteries: religious or natural mysteries, death, birth, the future, the past, cosmogony, void.

I am a master of hallucinations.

Listen! . . .

I possess every talent! – There is no one here and there is someone. I do not wish to compromise my riches. – Shall it be negro songs, houri dances? Shall I disappear diving in search of *the ring*? Shall I? I shall make gold, remedies.

It is interesting to note here how Rimbaud maintains the theme of 'Je est un autre' by a reaffirmation of duality. 'There is no one here and there is someone.' It comes back to the primary assertion of imaginative inquiry: 'Who am I: Who are we?' There is no answer to the polarized question of self-identity, so poetry exists as the ongoing dialogue with the unknowable. There are no answers and in time the questions become translated into lyric tangents and create the fictions we take for truth.

At the time of writing *Une saison en enfer* Rimbaud was physically exhausted and nervously delirious. Above all he was utterly alone. There was no one and nothing between him and his subject. His exposure was total. If there were any solace, it was in the physical relief of masturbation and in the realization that the big open spaces were calling to him again.

In 'Matin' Rimbaud looks back on a childhood like no other, but one which in its insatiable quest for experience encountered a precipitate halt in its confrontation with the world of social values. Rimbaud typifies the form of poetic idealism that is rebuffed by the impositions of bureaucracy, the unmediated jolt of insisting that disciplined employment should follow on directly from school, the attempt to collectivize rather than individualize, in short, all the deleterious principles governing manipulative ideologies, in the West or East. What the system induces in a young poet is FEAR. How can one gifted with the imagination stand out against the conglomerate? The individual is threatened with poverty, ill health and ostracism as a consequence of pursuing a vocation.

Did I not have *once upon a time* a delightful childhood, heroic, fabulous, to be written on sheets of gold – too lucky! Through what crime, through what error, have I deserved my present weakness? You who say that animals sob from grief, that the sick despair, that the dead have bad dreams, try to relate my fall and my sleep. I can explain myself no better than the vagrant with his incessant *Pater* and *Ave Maria*. *I do not know how to speak!*

Rimbaud speaks of a 'fall', a displacement, a discontinuity. He is like someone who has run out of light. The symptoms of drug withdrawal are prominent here; he tells of exhaustion and his 'sleep'. The dispiriting lethargy that comes from what must have been a drastic break with hashish and opium. There were no substitutes: no methadone, no valium. He had to live through paranoia, physical convulsion, the solitary suffering of a mind intent on a radical break with the past.

... When shall we journey beyond the beaches and the mountains, to salute the birth of the new work, the new wisdom, the flight of tyrants and demons, the end of superstition – the first! – to worship – Christmas on earth!

It is the impassioned question of the visionary poet who aspires to see the instatement of imaginative reality. If the poet could awake from a dream to find it materialized, he would have re-created the universe. And it is this hope which is at the heart of romanticism. This is the morning that Rimbaud would have known. It is the 'Matin' of his poem. The dawn that comes after the long watches of the night; the alchemical transmutation of black into red and gold, night into day. The completion of the work. But here it is not that at all: the longed-for morning remains a vision.

And Rimbaud awoke to a dawn without faith. Having summarily dismissed 'the bastard wisdom of the Koran', he is no more disposed to thinking that Christianity offers a way of truth. Rimbaud's nature revolted against comfort, his innate restiveness, his need to use himself as a source of experimentation and discovery, rather than rely on formulated doctrine to implant a faith inside him, made him the great uncompromising rebel that he carried into his poetry. And how do we greet the morning?

We assume the ordinary of what could be imagined as the advent of the true day – the manifestation of heaven or the imagination on earth.

And it is always there as a possibility. We have come to think of the dawn as confirmation of our own and the world's continuity. Drugged by coffee, insensible to the dawn – the bringer of light – we take our orientation on trust. Yet for Rimbaud the true morning involves radical transformation. It involves a break with the old day and the celebration of the new. It is like waking up to find no separation between one's dream and reality. We have at last arrived. But where does one go after that? One has stepped into a space that others do not occupy. Everything blazes, a dewdrop is an emerald with a foetus inside, the air opens out like pages of an atlas that have never been seen before, the ordinary house and shop on the corner are transformed into components of the new city, breath releases blossom and words are incantation, but what to do with the place and how to describe it? It should be visible to everyone, but it isn't. One has walked out of one's self and entered a new dimension. The change-over is bewildering but true. The poet always knew it would happen; but the materialists will call the actuality of vision madness.

There is in all visionary poetry from Blake onwards, through the Romantics and in particular Shelley, right up to the futuristic worlds envisaged in the novels of J.G. Ballard, an acceptance that imaginative reality is truth. There is no question of the elaboration of a fiction to support a theory. On the contrary it is material reality that is made to look dubious and inhibitive. But such a literature is still viewed with hostile suspicion by those who see the imagination as a subversive faculty more aligned with sensory disturbance than the discovery of the lost kingdom.

We go there in rags and we are transformed into gold. The way is open to those who have ditched the credential of reason. And the realization of having made the journey comes from the notion of suffering. The men in big cars are heading for their ordinary day, the one in which money is considered to represent advancement. If they see the likes of a Rimbaud on the road to somewhere else, their response is one of condescending contempt for drop-outs. Poets do not work, so what of them?

But Rimbaud's morning lives in a parallel universe. It belongs to a dimension we reach by a leap into the unknown, in the same way as we are startled on making contact with an animal. The experience has taken us somewhere else. In the latter case it is a reversion to the primal that activates the connection; man realizes his animalistic origins. In the former state, the awareness that the kingdom has been located is an ecstatic realization which desperately needs to be communicated to the world, but very often isn't. The poet's frustration is that the imaginative province he has discovered with such generative excitement remains uninhabited by readers.

Rimbaud might have ridden down the road on a lion's back, his eyes fixed on the future, but no one would have seen him. As it was, he gave voice to 'The song of heaven, the marching of nations'. And above all he waged war on all systems; he revolted against his youthful ideals – his belief in beauty and poetry had brought him nothing but rejection and suffering. The writing of *Une saison en enfer* effectively scorched everything that remained of his youth. It was as if Rimbaud had to set fire to the surrounding countryside. Fire was his retribution: he must have hoped to incinerate his past and begin again. Only there was a deficit, and it was one of time and experience. He could not undo what he had known. He was marked. An alchemical pact made with poetry leaves an ineradicable scar. If Rimbaud had pursued his fanaticism, he might have ended up like that other sun worshipper, Harry Crosby, who had black suns tattooed on the soles of his feet.

In 'Adieu' his valediction is not only to poetry but to the alchemical sun. It is a leave-taking that involves the creation of a new poetic cosmos and not the invocation of one the poet is prepared dramatically to disown.

Autumn already! – But why regret an eternal sun, if we are committed to the discovery of divine light – far from those who die according to the seasons.

Autumn. Our ship hanging in motionless fog turns towards

the port of poverty, the huge city under a sky flecked with fire and mud. Ah! the rotten rags, the rain-soaked bread, the drunkenness, the thousand loves which crucified me! She will never have done, that ghoul queen of millions of souls and dead bodies *and who will be judged*! I see myself again, my skin ravaged by mud and plague, my hair and my armpits alive with worms, and still bigger worms in my heart, lying stretched out among strangers without age, without feeling. . . . I could have died there. . . . It is an insufferable memory! I detest poverty.

And I fear winter because it is the season of comfort!

Rimbaud affirms with invincible courage the power of the inner light. Autumn cannot reach those 'committed to the discovery of divine light'. The poet lives in a condition of timelessness; illumination centres itself in the word. Had he not already invented colours for the vowels? The alchemical transmutation was effecting itself now in his spiritual autumn which was full of the red and gold permutations of the work. He had used his body as the alchemical vessel. Out of his long night in hell – his occupation of the nigredo – had come a ferocious light guarded by lions that lay down around the furnace.

The imaginary city, one of poverty and disease which Rimbaud evokes, is still another of the inner cities that belong to his visionary itinerary. One could draw up a Rimbaud cosmography, a map as fabulous and original as those used by the Venetian sea-kings in their voyage into the speculative unknown. Rimbaud provides a city for an inner state. Where did he see it? Was it in London in his months of derelict suffering, or now in his delirious confrontation with mania. It is a place of disease and squalor, Rimbaud is imposing reality – his own rotten clothes and rain-sodden bread and cheap wine – on hallucination, the masturbatory fantasy of 'the thousand loves which crucified me!' An image powerful for its disturbing sado-masochistic overtones, its suggestion of anonymous sex and its concomitant register of disease which has come to characterize the condition of our world ravaged by Aids as we approach the millennium. Rimbaud sees himself in a form of necrotic decay; there are worms in his hair, his armpits, but, worse than that, they have taken to tunnelling through his heart. In his orgiastic exposure he finds himself amongst strangers who appear to have neither age nor feeling. 'I could have died there. . . .' In Rimbaud the interchange between inner and outer is indivisible; what is imagined and what has been experienced is inseparable from immediacy.

There was no one to live up to now, other than himself. Verlaine was stuck in prison, Delahaye was working in Charleville, Paris was light years ago; his family were rustics preoccupied with the harvest. Probably he lacked even a mirror in which to check his face. He was who? A fist raised against the sky. Someone who had lost track of himself. He had thrown himself against the barriers of infinity. He had adopted madness; he had shouted in the streets, vomited the drug into gutters which blazed back at him, sapphire and emerald. He had left a trail of wanderings. It was all connected to his umbilical like a spider's silk threads. Each road, each field, each alley, each room he had lived in. When he breathed in under stress, his whole past punched him in the solar plexus. Withdrawal is like that. But there was vision, and his poetry rises to salute the unknown, to embrace the future.

– Sometimes I see in the sky endless beaches covered with white celebratory nations. A huge golden vessel, above me, waves its multicoloured flags in the morning breeze. I have created all festivities, all triumphs, all dramas. I have tried to invent new flowers, new stars, new flesh, new tongues. I believed I had acquired supernatural powers. Well! I have to bury my imagination and my memories! A fine reputation as an artist and story-teller swept away!

I! I who called myself magus or angel, exempt from all morality, am thrown back to the earth, with a task to pursue, and hard reality to embrace! Peasant!

A whole new poetry begins with passages like these from *Une saison en enfer*. Rimbaud's vision of a future world is in the sky. It is there he sees the endless beaches of which voyagers had gone in search across the seas. The ship likewise is in the sky. The imagination defies gravity: we are on the threshold of surrealism, which is a word for the natural order of things as they are encountered by the imagination. And there is no abatement to Rimbaud's originality. Even in describing his past achievements he is inventing a new poetry. And it was not that he tried to create new flowers, stars, flesh, tongues: he actually succeeded in doing so. Most poets readily look for limitations, a defined order they can either describe or to which they can apply a metaphysics. Rimbaud's way is to eliminate the preconceived and try for the impossible. A poet must be bored in order to create, and by that I mean at odds with the accepted nature of the appearance of things. The limitless must replace the circumscribed. Visual retrieval must go beyond seeing and activate irreconcilables in a manner that leads to a continuous re-creation of the universe. Close your eyes for five minutes and the world you took on trust should start to disappear, until you are left only with ideas about things. Then the ideas should recede and the imagination take over. The poet begins with the latter premiss as the basis for reality.

Rimbaud has chosen to bury his imagination like treasure. It is an action devoid of all self-pity, and it is one of the great moments of self-abnegation in the history of poetry. At eighteen he can look back on his achievements as a thing of the past. His creative life has been so intense that three years seem like a millennium. Little wonder he could spit over his shoulder at those who knew nothing of this initiatory rite into the psychological hells of the underworld. Rimbaud is the shaman born into industrialism. He is in his own words 'the great criminal', because he trafficks between worlds. He despises poverty, but his gifts are inconvertible into anything but poetry. 'Weeping I stared at gold and could not drink' he tells us in 'Alchimie du verbe'. His correspondence is with magic. He would have agreed with Aleister Crowley that the imaginative presences are of a higher order than their human counterparts. They comprise aliens, extraterrestrials, daimons, whatever term best fits their physically unrealizable state. 'My observation of the Universe', writes Crowley in *Magick without Tears*, 'convinces me that there are beings of intelligence and power of a far higher quality than anything we can conceive of as human; that they are not necessarily based on the cerebral and nervous structure that we know; and that the one and only chance for mankind to advance as a whole is for individuals to make contact with such Beings.'

Rimbaud's contact with the informing agents of the imagination is the subject of *Une saison en enfer*, as it is of much of *Les Illuminations*. In this, his revocation of poetry, he prepares to let them go. He is seen exorcizing his childhood ideals, and in doing so he projects them on the future. They are there for the enlightened in the twentieth century to use. One might say that every true poet is possessed by one of the psychic presences that Rimbaud disowned. He left them in the air as potentiated fall-out.

Yes, the new hour is redoubtable.

For I can say that victory is mine: the gnashing of teeth, the hissing of fire, the voice of disease abates. All filthy memories are erased. My last regrets take to their heels – envy of beggars, scoundrels, friends of death, all sorts of backward creatures. Damned, if I avenged myself!

We must be absolutely modern.

No hymns: I must hold on to my gain. A hard night! Dried blood smokes on my face, and I have nothing behind me, except that twisted tree! . . . Spiritual battle is as brutal as the battle of men; but the vision of justice is God's pleasure alone.

However, it is the eve. Let us welcome all influxes of strength and real tenderness. And at dawn, armed with burning patience, we shall enter magnificent cities.

What was I saying about a friendly hand! One advantage is that I can laugh at old lying loves and strike shame into those couples – I have seen the women's hell down there; – and I shall be free *to possess truth in one body and soul.*

What makes for the tension here is that the poet is writing from the same source as he is renouncing. Rimbaud has never been more volatile or rich with his gift. It is an act of cataclysmic vengeance on his part to leave massive reserves of poetry unrealized. By the nature of creativity, one work leads directly to another, and where the barriers between the two exist they are largely arbitrary. A poem or a novel is brought to conclusion only so that the withheld energies may be redirected into another work. But for Rimbaud this is not the case. The constrained momentum is not to be redistributed. It is to be left unlocalized. And what happens when poetry is deprived of an outlet? It becomes a source of disturbance and psychosomatic illness. Negating his creative impetus, Rimbaud was to end up as a pariah, an unsuccessful trader burnt and disfigured by the hardships of his desert life until he was another Rimbaud. The unrecognizable simulacrum of the poet.

Rimbaud's 'victory' as he describes it seems to be one of having survived withdrawal symptoms. He has come through. The inner torment and cacophony of shrieks has abated. His identification with criminals, vagrants, mental and physical drop-outs, which had begun with 'Les Poëtes de sept ans', has been replaced by the credo: 'We must be absolutely modern.' His night has been a long one. Who can say when it was begun? Poetry messes up one's conception of time, it involves one in a series of distorted flash-backs and flash-forwards. Was it in Paris, Brussels or last night sleeping out in the barn that Rimbaud had acquired dried blood on his face? His inner battle had raged in torment for so long that he knew now only exhaustion, the certainty that a phase in his life had reached completion. And the cities of which he had dreamt were awaiting him somewhere in the dawn.

Rimbaud's family had turned to the fruit harvest, but still he refused to help. Autumn was here with dead leaves crackling underfoot on the parched soil, nothing and no one for miles. He had undertaken a work of solitary genius; but his suffering was nothing to the blank that would greet his book. Perhaps out of pity for his ruined condition, and in the hope that the book would lend some financial security to her itinerant son, Madame Rimbaud advanced Arthur the money necessary to have the poem printed as a plaquette in Brussels by Jacques Poot, 37 Rue Aux-Choux. Five hundred copies were to be printed, of which Rimbaud was to receive ten complimentaries. A white cover with simple black typography. No ostentation. No detraction from the seriousness of the text. The work was dated April–August 1873. Rimbaud was still eighteen.

Post-Delirium

That Rimbaud went to Brussels in the last week of October 1873 to collect his author's copies of *Une saison en enfer* from the printer, and that the entire edition with the exception of ten or twelve copies was impounded owing to his failure to meet the printer's bill, does not concern us here. It is part of literary history. What happened beyond this point has become the subject of speculative biography. Rimbaud managed to leave a copy for Verlaine at the prison of the Petits Carmes, and the copies he circulated in Paris went unnoticed. He had already alienated himself from the Parnassians, and the hysterical nature of his affair with Verlaine, leading to the latter's imprisonment, was the subject of moral turpitude among those who saw Rimbaud as an impostor, a youth intent on ruining his older friend.

But delirium: hallucinated consciousness, schizoid dissociation, manic overreach – call it what one will, Rimbaud is the celebrant of modern consciousness. It is in the likes of Hart Crane, Antonin Artaud, Robert Desnos, André Breton, Aimé Cesaire, Federico Garcia Lorca in his New York poems, and in the visual art of Munch, Soutine, Ernst, Bacon and Pollock that Rimbaud resurfaces. The chaos out of which all these artists create is an inherited delirium. Rimbaud's unfinished work lives on as a current. It is centred in the permanent storm that hangs over the twentieth century. And his legacy will go on being part of the creative future for as long as there is a world in which poetry functions.

What does it mean to be dead? We cannot ask Rimbaud. His

life is the story of someone who overtook himself at each critical juncture in his development. He refused to outstay himself. His unrealized past is always the potential future.

Being hooked on poetry is a terrible thing. If the need is complicated by drugs, we have a powerful double addiction. Rimbaud, the poet, choked on himself. He wanted to bite so deeply into inner experience that he became the snake asphyxiating on its tail.

Sometimes I imagine Rimbaud as a naked figure running from wall to wall of an empty house. The building is white and has no windows. The interior walls are black, bare except for the obscene slogans he has written on them in blood and excrement. When he came across this house in the wasteland, he crawled into it hoping it would offer shelter. The night he intended to stay lengthened to infinity. Time had ceased to exist; his clock was mania. It is like that when you are in extreme states of altered consciousness. It is easier to be stretched out the wrong way than it is to return. And sometimes it seems easier to crawl out of your skin, only there is nowhere to go after that.

Rimbaud feared containment. Going into the desert was a means of avoiding the threat of institutionalized madness. It is time at last to hear the voice of Artaud:

And what is an authentic madman? It is a man who has elected to go mad, in the sense in which society understands the term, rather than compromise for a certain superior idea of human honour. That is why society has had all those of whom it wanted to rid itself, against whom it wanted to defend itself, because they had refused to become its accomplices in certain acts of debasement, condemned to be strangled in its asylums. For a madman is primarily someone to whom society did not want to listen and whom it wanted to prevent from uttering unbearable truths. (*Le Théâtre et son double*)

Delirium is not so much a state as a means of attempting to overtake it. The central theme of *Une saison en enfer* is announced in Délires I and II: the autobiographical inferno of his relationship with Verlaine and 'L'histoire d'une de mes folies' – the alchemical nature of his poetic experiments. Both pieces of writing are extraordinary for their attempt to overtake the immediacy of their subject.

If there is a pulse-beat in paper, it will be heard in *Une saison en enfer*. The poem is a paper cell. Rimbaud's *délire* resists imprisonment by words. His acceleration is manic. Mad he wants to be beyond madness.

And that is the direction of fearlessness, the poetic equivalent of running towards the heat-flash. The experience is beyond language. It is post-somatic. If it has a voice, it is in the expression of an Artaudian shriek. In 'Mauvais sang' Rimbaud reached the stage whereby music, the frenzied rhythm of primitive dance – 'Hunger, thirst, shrieks, dance, dance, dance, dance!' – had come to replace words. He had left poetry behind him. When he operated, it was right on the frontier between language and the incomprehensible. Between implosion and hallucination.

If he stood still long enough on the road, looking at his shadow, he could project the one who would come after him. A stock-still noon. The sun black. No one around. The wind trapped in poplars. Letting something go means constructing a future without it. His was sand. Who was the poet coming on the road? No one. There would be echoes. Rimbaud returning in another's imbalance. His voice is always there. It says: 'Go to the edge or don't begin.' It says: 'The ego is a sickness. Poetry lives independent of coteries and publication.' It says: 'Burn. There is no other way.'

Rimbaud spent the money his mother gave him for the publication of *Une saison en enfer*. He needed to. He had spent his life in rags, in deprivation. He had sold everything, including his body. And he despised poverty. He had been humiliated in his travels, his clothes stank. He had turned his acute sensitivity to his very real suffering into an intransigent arrogance. He had believed that collective materialism was no more than a sugar carnival skull. He had broken his fist on the misrepresentation. The mob had reviled him as they would an epileptic.

There is a screen between poetry and its conversion into money, and no relationship between the two. Creativity responds to an autonomous inner drive. The opposite to which it is attracted is its likeness – TRUTH. But poets need money, for their vulnerability asks protection. From the nineteenth century onwards that help which should have been directed towards the committed has been appropriated by the popular, the journalistic, the maffia attached to vested literary interests whose representatives are intent on the subversion of truth.

Paranoia is a term invested with pejoratively pathological undertones. In the Rimbaudian sense, it means a healthy apprehension of the individual shadowed by a hostile collective. What else can the poet do but shriek? Rimbaud asked nothing more than that his vision of the world be encountered as a reality. Jung says:

> . . . If a world-wide consciousness could arise that all division and all antagonism are due to the splitting of opposites in the psyche, then one could really know where to attack. But if even the smallest and most personal stirrings of the individual soul – so insignificant in themselves – remain as unconscious and unrecognized as they have hitherto, they will go on accumulating and produce mass groupings and mass movements which cannot be subjected to reasonable control or manipulated to a good end. All direct efforts to do so are no more than shadow boxing, the most infatuated by illusion being the gladiators themselves.   (*The Undiscovered Self*)

And Jung like Freud is a product of Rimbaud. Both men are the psychological interpreters of the psychic cataclysm experienced by Lautréamont and Rimbaud. Not madness, but the realization that the psyche is an unmapped continent. Rimbaud's deep soundings in the interior had revealed states in which the primal was still predominant. Areas locatable to the poetic imagination where reason, gravity, predictability were all subservient to a highly organized disorder. In 'Soir historique' from *Les Illuminations* Rimbaud had written of the domestic and universal in revolt in a confrontation no less strange than Lautréamont's meeting of an umbrella and sewing-machine.

And some evening, for instance, the simple tourist, retiring from our economic horrors, finds the hands of the master have brought to life the harpsichord of the fields; they play cards at the bottom of the pond, a mirror evocative of queens and of favourites; there are saints, sails, threads of harmony, and chromatic legends, in the sunset.

... No! The moment of the bath-house, of seas boiling to foam, of underground conflagrations, of the planet carried off, of subsequent exterminations, certainties indicated with so little malice by the Bible and the Norns and which are signs for the serious man to watch. – Though the entire effect will be hardly a legend!

So much happens here that had never before occurred in poetry. Playing cards at the bottom of a pond, a harpsichord strung by the wind in the fields, the planet getting blown off – great events of the imagination such as these are treated with a spontaneity that transforms hallucination into reality. *Les Illuminations* is the Book of Reality. No apology is needed for the true nature of things.

Rimbaud is a cosmographer. He reinvents the universe. Seeing has become so much a condition of preconception (we take on trust the idea of the thing we see) that we all long for a flaw, a rift in the seam, a divide through which we may apprehend an altered state of the universe.

I am so accustomed to hallucination, that watching a tree break into fire in a scarlet field under an emerald sky is one of a thousand visual metamorphoses I may encounter before and during the writing of a poem. While still a schoolboy I grew bored with the limitations of colour perceived by the human eye and so imagined the world as I might paint it. Mid-afternoon. I could sit on black sands under a violent cerise sky. If I wanted the sea to be white with the odd red and blue sail pricking up a cat's ear on the skyline, so it turned out according to that composition. And eventually what begins as self-induced, asserts an autonomous function. The poet lives through the creation of a private mythology which becomes in time the way that others learn to see an alternative or parallel universe. Hallucinogens like LSD are not necessary to the discovery of a visually heightened universe. If they are used, it is for no more than tincturing, adding tone to a palette already vitalized and set by the imagination.

Changing one's perception of the world should be as easy as switching programmes on a television set. Now I am in a meadow, now I am in a street, sunflowers brushing my neck, now I am floating through the sky. . . . I can be anywhere through a modulation of psychic energy.

Rimbaud comes into focus again. His lip is split; blood is caked on his right index finger. A loop of saliva is twisted around his collar. Did he have a fit, back there off the road? His eyes are hugely dilated. Maybe he is perturbed with what I have just written. He wants to pulp the paragraph with his raw fist. Where does anything come from and why?

I can repeat it, only differently. Rimbaud is at the London docks, sitting by himself watching the commerce on the river. Blue, brown and grey river and sky colours mingle. A shaft of sunlight crosses his left knee. His right profile is in shadow. He is thinking that poetry has ruined him. It is while focusing on the naked torso of a West Indian docker that he decides his life lies elsewhere, that man's back will remain the source of his decision. He has thought into its hollow. He has watched the subtle kundalini of the spine. He has suffered for the animal labour of the man. He will never know his name, and yet their lives intersected at a crucial point.

Rimbaud comes into focus again. This time his skin is blistered black from the desert sun. He is emaciated; his body is like a junkie's. No flesh on the bones. His face hollowed in to follow the bone structure of the skull. He carries a gun. He would blow the back out of anything. He would like to shoot the image of him I carry in my head.

Rimbaud, detail of a gouache by
Fantin-Latour, 1872

Paul Verlaine at the time when he and Rimbaud
were friends

The house at 34 Howland Street, where Rimbaud and Verlaine lived in London in 1872

Young London coachman, drawn
by Rimbaud in 1872

Rimbaud in 1872, drawn by
Verlaine

Rue Campagne-Première, Paris, where Rimbaud lodged in the hotel in 1872

JEREMY REED

Rimbaud and the Sand Leopard

Wind spitting the red sand in my eyes my
mouth. The poems I wrote on the desert's face
are gone: the bitty black grains pour
into another undulating dune.
The sun's too close. I hear it roar at noon.

The road I took from Tajoura to Ankober
still burns up molten in my head.
The camels whistle; packs loaded with arms.
The shrunken salt lake's stagnant bed
contains another holocaustal sun,
and when I woke at night the flames were red
in which my poems burnt. They thought me mad
and pointed to nothing but sand,
no ash, no scattered books, no char:
the morning star.

The girl I brought from the interior
to console me in the ferocious waste
of youth and time, changed into a white sand leopard,
and stalked me, an assassin or a mirage,
hot breath and claws opening my chest at night,
and in the morning, blood-spots on the floor,
my body thin as a hollow bamboo,
my eyes punched in by the drilling white light.

And Djami, he alone
hears how the poem sings from a hot stone.
A snake drinks from my leather mouth;
and are we moving again? always South
into the sun's eye. Vultures, warring tribes.
My leg an amputated bone.

I think if I went out into the dawn

the leopard's tongue might lick me clean
before the kill. In death I'll meet the youth
who wrote my poems; the one with mop-hair
I left crumpled with rage in our provincial square.

The versions of Rimbaud which follow are intended as imitations, in the sense that Robert Lowell employed the term, and not as literal translations.

J.R.

The Drunken Boat

(Le Bateau ivre)

No longer guided by haulers, I felt
the current chase me down sluggish rivers.
Yelping redskins had made human targets,
nailed them to stakes and cut out their livers.

I was indifferent to every crew,
carriers of English cottons, Flemish wheat.
My haulers dead, the uproars extinguished,
the waters left me to a steady beat.

Last winter, more dumbstruck than a child's mind
I ran into the ferocious rip-tides.
The surf lashed me; loosened peninsulas
were like white thunder smashing at my sides.

The storm celebrated my sea vigils.
Lighter than a cork I danced on the waves,
the big rollers which distribute the drowned.
Ten nights. Lighthouses marking sailors' graves.

Sweeter than waspish apples to children,
the green water oozed through my pinewood hull,
scouring the vomit splashes and blue wine.
Rudder and planks were gashed by a sea-bull.

Later, I found the Poem of the Sea,
infused with starlight and latescent spray,
and nosed through green azure where a drowned man
rolled up and down and sometimes seemed to stay.

It's there, the bitter red of love ferments,
stronger than alcohol, madder than lyres,
slow rhythms heard around the break of day
light up the deep blue with delirium's fires.

I've known skies split by lightnings, waterspouts,

surf and the looping currents, evening too,
and dawn exalted like a flock of doves.
I've seen the things man thought he saw and knew.

I've watched the low sun packed with mystic scars,
its long violet clots burning out in space,
resembling manic actors on the boards,
waves running blinds up across the surface.

I've dreamt of a green night with dazzled snows,
a kiss rising from the deeps to the sky,
the circulation of all unknown saps,
yellow and blue phosphor singing in the sea's eye.

I've followed in gestative months the swell
running like hysterical cows to smash
their violent panic on the reefs. I've sensed
the snouting sea-herd stilled by a star's flash.

I've struck against amazing Floridas
where flowers are panther's eyes in human skin,
and rainbows dropped down as the bridle reins
keeping the glaucous sea-horizons in.

I've seen enormous swamps ferment, fish traps
where a Leviathan rots on the beach.
Water avalanching out of a calm,
cataracts shrieking in their overreach!

Glaciers, silver suns, waves shot through red,
I've seen wrecks in brown gulfs, stood upside-down,
and giant serpents devoured by vermin
smoke with black scent in a knotted tree crown.

I should have liked to point out to children
gold dolphins singing as they broke the wave,
while spindrift flowers jostled my driftings,
and winds beat like wings over the sea's grave.

Sometimes a victim, coursing between poles,
the sea whose groundswell lifted with the breeze
carried black flowers with yellow suckers
and dragged me like a woman on her knees . . .

Almost an island, with its squalling birds
high over beaches, I rocked on the deep,
or sailed on, seeing through my smashed rigging
drowned men somersault backwards into sleep.

I ran, a boat conversant with sea-caves,
blasted by the storm into birdless air;
I whose sodden boards, taking in water,
would have attracted no one to its flare.

Free, smoking and risen from violet fogs,
I who bored through the red sky like a wall
carried preserves for good poets, blue jam,
azure snot, sunlight fattened to a ball.

I shot, speckled with small electric moons,
a wild plank, black sea-horses by my side,
while July furnaced down burning funnels
and ultramarine skies fumed in the tide . . .

I who trembled, hearing on the skyline,
rampant Behemoths, a whirlpool's shut eye,
spun on blue spaces, longing for Europe,
its parapets crowding into the sky.

I've seen spiral galaxies and islands
whose delirious skies open out to death.
And from those bottomless nights, golden birds,
will you rise at last on the future's breath?

But truly I've known too much pain. The dawns
are inconsolable, the moon a scar,
love's left me disconnected, spaced on drugs,
I need to sink rock bottom, go that far.

If there's one water in Europe I need,
it's the black cold pool where a child will try
sometimes at evening to launch a toy boat,
its structure lighter than a butterfly.

I can no longer, lit up by the surf,
sit in the wake of cotton boats, nor keep
appointment with riotous flags, nor dive
under prison ships steering for the deep.

Vowels

(Voyelles)

A black, E white, I red, U green, O blue:
I shall tell of vowels and their arcane birth.
A, black brilliance of flies matting the earth,
fidgeting around stench, and out of view

the shadow gulfs. E, white vapours and tents,
glacier splinters, snow-kings, cow-parsley;
I, purples, spat blood, lips inquiringly
framed in a smile or drunken indictment.

U, cycles, the vibration of green seas,
serene meadows dotted with cows, or lines
mapped on a forehead versed in alchemy;

O, a trumpet shrieking out of deep skies,
the void in which planets and angels shine.
– O Omega, the violet ray from his eyes.

The Sleeper in the Valley

(Le Dormeur du val)

A green hollow, the river's voice points there,
and seethes through grasses, madly pawing free
in silver tatters. The sun fires the air
above the mountain; rays flood the valley.

A young soldier lies open mouthed, head back,
pillowed on a bed of blue watercress,
asleep, where tall ferns overcrowd the track.
The sun-warmed grass affords him ease from stress.

His feet thrust in red flowers, he sleeps. His smile
is like a sick child's, it is infantile.
He is stone-cold, nail-heads flash from his soles.

Flower scents no longer break into his rest,
he sleeps in sunlight, one hand on his breast.
In his right side are two red bullet-holes.

Seven-year-old Poets

(Les Poëtes de sept ans)

Dutifully shutting up the copy-book,
the mother, with a proud and imperious look,
ignored her child's contemptuous disdain,
his blue eyes flashing, his face scored with spots.

All day he studied in a sweat, and crammed,
but through his effortless facility
dark fissures showed; a sour hypocrisy.
In corridors, their mildewed papers blotched
by damp, he'd stick his tongue out, and fists jammed
into his groin, see lights behind his eyes
reveal a pattern. When a door opened
admitting lamplight, they could see him high
on the stairway, contained and out of reach. . . .
In summer, cowed, complacent like a fish
he'd meditate in the latrines and wish
he was a hermit on a coral beach.

In winter, he'd lie up behind the house,
buried in clay, feet stretched against a wall
and watch a cold moon whiten the garden.
He'd force his eyes until visions appeared,
and hear the creak of rotten trellises.
The friends he chose as his accomplices
were stringy, poor, pink-eyed and cretinous,
who hid yellow and black grubby fingers
coated with mud in threadbare, patched-up clothes.
They spoke with gaps, these prematurely old
village idiots, and if his mother caught
him out in these friendships, and if she knew
the depths of his concern, she said nothing.
Lies come easily if your eyes are blue.

At seven he began to write novels
about lives in the desert, liberty,

forests, suns, riverbanks, wastelands. His mind
was prompted by the magazines he'd find
depicting Spanish and Italian girls
in poses that had his cheeks burn with fire.
And when, brown-eyed, short-skirted and frisky,
the little girl of eight who lived next door
would roughly jump on him without panties
and pin him in a corner, he would bite
her bottom, hold her face down to the floor
until she beat him black and blue, and he
could taste her skin. It lasted all the night.

He feared December Sundays, the ennui
of sitting with his hair greased back, reading
a Bible with its cabbage-green edges.
Nightly, dreams pushed him out on cliff-ledges;
he hated God, but loved the grimy men
he saw at evening return to suburbs,
where mad performing artists and vendors
were crowded round like monsters in a den.
He dreamt of prairies, the earth's rising scent
and golden puberties, love on a plain
rushed by the quick wind and laid flat again.

He relished the dark things in life, and sat
in his bare shuttered room, the ceiling blue,
inhaling its sodden humidity.
The novel that he read took up the theme
of heavy ochre skies, flooded forests,
flesh-petalled flowers open in astral woods.
– Then cataclysm, collapse, vertigo,
neighbourhood noises carried from the street.
He lay stretched out on a raw canvas bale,
hunched, tense, already breaking into sail.

Faun's Head

(Tête de faune)

In foliage, a dense green flecked with gold,
tentative leaves on fire with gorgeous flowers,
in that green heart a vivid kiss smoulders,
exploding through the sumptuous tapestry.

A startled faun abruptly shows his eyes
and bites the scarlet flowers with white teeth.
Stained as the crimson sediment of wine,
his mouth opens in laughter on a leaf.

And when he breaks for cover like a squirrel,
his outcry still vibrates in every tree,
and you can see as a bullfinch triggers
the gold woodland crown close like a whirlpool.

Saarebrück

(L'Eclatante Victoire de Sarrebrück)

Loaded with blue and gold, a demigod,
the Emperor commands the middle ground,
his saddle posture's stiff as a ramrod,
he hardly jolts when his horse paws a mound.

The conscripts group around a gilded tent
and a red cannon; they rise drowsily.
Pitou salutes the historic moment,
and greets the Emperor with 'Victory!'

Dumanet leans on his rifle like a cane,
a peasant farmer taking stock of rain,
he shouts 'The Emperor!' to a stony ring

of faces, only wine would make them sing. . . .
Boquillon, flat out in blue, shifts his butt,
and sneeringly quips 'Emperor of what?'

The Lice Hunters

(Les Chercheuses de poux)

The child's head throbs; its red flush sparks with pain;
he dreams of faces behind streaming veils
before he sits up, his two big sisters
are by his bed, long fingers, silver nails.

They take the child to a dormer window,
a flower garden swims in the blue air.
The dew silvers, as they begin their search,
slow fingers probing his unruly hair.

Enticing, intimate, their breath vibrates,
its rose-scent has him shiver; now they miss,
and now they catch, he hears saliva drawn
lightly over red lips designed to kiss.

Their eyelashes beat like frenetic moths,
electric fingers set his blood on fire,
he lies submissively, his hair crackles;
beneath their sovereign nails the lice expire.

Entranced, and lazy as though dulled by wine,
or the harmonica's deluding wail
the child feels in their caresses the first
awakenings of a future lifting sail.

On the Road

(Ma bohème – Fantaisie)

I'd take to the road, my fists thrust inside
torn pockets, my threadbare coat grown ideal.
I walked under the sky, the Muse my bride.
I dreamt of making my brilliant loves real.

My trousers gaped from disrepair, my shirt
was buttonless; my pursuit was the line
I'd strike into a lyric. The ground hurt.
I lay at night exposed to cold star-shine.

On autumn evenings sitting by a ditch
I listened to the stars and felt the dew
cold on my forehead burnt to fever-pitch

by a strong wine. I acted out my part
playing the lyre on laces threaded through
the busted boot I nursed beneath my heart.

At the Green Inn

(Au Cabaret-Vert)

For a whole week I ripped my boots to shreds,
scuffing the stones. I entered Charleroi,
and at the Green Inn asked for buttered bread
and half-cooled ham. The waitress was a toy.

Happy, I stuck my legs out underneath
the green table and studied the artless
designs of the wallpaper, then the dress
of the big-breasted girl, no straps, a sheath

– a kiss wouldn't scare her vivacity –
she brought me my request, and smilingly
let her eyes dance upon the coloured plate,

pink and white ham spiked with clove of garlic,
and filled my beer-mug, I could hear it tick,
a sunbeam lit the froth's heady gold spate.

Hunger

('Faim', *Une saison en enfer*)

If I have a taste
it's for the earth and stones.
I always feed on air,
rock, coal and iron.

My hungers circulate
elect fields of sound,
drain the bright poison
of convolvuli.

Eat the broken pebbles,
old church stone,
boulders left by floods,
bread sown in grey valleys.

———————

The wolf howled under the leaves,
spitting out bright feathers
of his feast of fowl:
like him I consume myself.

Lettuce, fruit
wait only to be picked;
but the hedge-spider
eats only violets.

Let me sleep! Let me simmer
on Solomon's altars.
The scum boils over the rust
and flows into the Cédron.

Finally, o happiness, o reason, I removed from the sky the
blue which is black, and I lived as a gold spark of cosmic light.
From joy, I adopted the most absurd and exaggerated modes of
expression:

It is found again!
What? Infinity.
It is the sea mixed
with the sun.

My eternal soul,
live your dream
despite the lonely night
and the flaming day.

So you free yourself
from human suffering,
common aspirations!
You fly off free . . .

– Always without hope
and no *orietur*.
Science and patience,
torture is sure.

No more tomorrow
satin starfire,
your resolute heat
is duty.

It is found again!
What? Infinity.
It is the sea mixed
with the sun.

Stupra: Three Scatological Sonnets

(Les Stupra)

1

Ancient beasts copulated on the run,
their glans coated with blood and excrement.
Our fathers puffed their big dicks out, displayed
their wrinkled foreskins and bark-grainy balls.

The medieval woman, angel or pig
asked for a lover with huge dimensions.
Even a Kléber, judging by his pants,
seemed to have debatable resources.

Man and the proudest mammals have one front;
their giant pricks are very like our own,
but a sterile period has struck, the horse

and the bull have bridled their white-hot heat,
and no one again will display genitals
in the woods where children invent first sex-games.

2

Our arse-holes are not theirs. Often I saw
men unbutton their pants behind a hedge,
and in those unembarrassed childhood baths
I studied the architecture of the arse.

Tight, and in most cases white, its easy curves
are formed by planes of muscles, and it's screened
by a network of hairs; for women it's a slit,
a groove black with tufted satin flowers.

A moving and wonderful inventiveness
of painted angels on a blue tableau
recalls the cheek where a smile indents flesh.

Oh! to be naked now, twitching for fun,
my head moving down on my friend's fat cock,
both of us whispering in ecstasy.

Obscure and wrinkled like a violet
it breathes, worn out and modest amongst moss,
still wet with love, laid up on the buttock's
curved incline to the tangled pit.

Threads hang like gossamers of milk, small tears
pushed back by a rebuffing wind
over small clots of reddish marl,
they lose themselves in droplets on the slopes.

In my dream my mouth sucked at the crack,
my soul, jealous of this wild coitus,
makes it a tearful place, lamenting nest.

It's the olive and the cajoling flute,
the tube from which heavenly praline flows,
feminine Canaan sticky with moisture.

CITY LIGHTS MAIL ORDER
Order books from our free catalog:

all books from
CITY LIGHTS PUBLISHERS
and more

write to:
CITY LIGHTS MAIL ORDER
261 COLUMBUS AVENUE
SAN FRANCISCO, CA 94133
or fax your request to
[415] 362-4921